Copyright 2016 by Jodi Rose
Inmate Sharing

Beverly, West Virginia
Like us on Facebook

I0467676

ISBN-13:
978-1533495600

ISBN-10:
1533495602

Inmate Sharing

Presents

"Locked Up"

From Both Sides of the Wire

VOL. 1

By. Jodi Rose

BS Criminal Justice, MS Higher Education w/emphasis in
Criminal Justice,
Certified Overcomers Recovery Support,
Jail & Prison Advocate and Volunteer

This book is dedicated to my son Michael who is currently incarcerated.

The inmates and their loved ones I communicate with on a daily basis.

My husband, children, and family, that have stood beside me and continues to, through the hardest times of my life, the current incarceration of my son.

To all my friends on "Incarcerated Sons, Daughters, Husbands, Wives, and Loved Ones of Felons support group on Facebook.

Most of all I want to thank God for giving me strength to endure the pain that goes with having loved one's that are incarcerated.

Many homes across America have been shattered by bad choices which resulted in being locked up, receiving sentences that takes mothers, fathers, sons, daughters, boyfriends, girlfriends, loved ones, away from their families. The majority of the time loved ones (I refer to them as LO's) encounter so much when they have a LO that gets "locked up". Some have never experienced it before where as others like myself have years of coping with the incarceration of loved ones.

Even if you are not the one to commit the crimes and be sentenced to do the time, still as a LO we are also "locked up". There are two sides to the wire, what I mean by that is there is the side for life as an inmate, then there is the other side; the loved one of the incarcerated. We both do the time, we all do the time, anyone involved does the time. Often we have no idea what to do, what to expect, where to turn. We feel so lonely, like we are all alone, although in reality 2.4 million are locked up, so think about how many LO's that would include if we added it up. More and more loved ones are becoming victims to the fact we are losing someone to the system. It is a very hard thing to deal with, to understand, to overcome. Some inmates are locked up for only a short time whereas others are doing 20,30,40 years and even life. Lock downs, segregation, chow hall, all the many things we hear from our LO's. This book will give you the words straight from inmates and their loved ones as to what life on both sides of the wire is like. Before we begin I would like to explain in a very short way why the incarceration rate is so out of control. Why 1 in every 28 children in America have an incarcerated parent, what has caused our CJ system to become a complete disaster?

Incarceration has been spreading like wild fire for years, according to a report recently released by Prison Policy discovered there are 2.3 million Americans being held in our criminal justice system. The United States currently has over 1700 state prisons, 102 Federal Facilities, 942 juvenile centers, and a whopping 3,283 county jails. Also, included are Native American jails, military prisons, immigration facilities, and private sector institutions. Regardless of the crimes our loved ones committed, the fact is they are being taken out of homes, away from family, jobs, their overall daily living for bad choices they have made. One in every 4 inmates are locked up for drug charges, yes being punished for being addicted. Over half a million people are doing time for drug offenses. You may wonder why incarceration is growing at such a fast pace. The dramatic growth of incarceration came when sentencing policies were changed in the 1980's to get tougher on crime. "The War on Drugs" was stemmed by president Nixon when his administration pushed for mandatory minimum sentencing; which forced judges to sentence offenders with minimum of 5,10,20,25 years to life for non-violent drug crimes. Also in 1971 Nixon placed marijuana in a Schedule One, which is the most restrictive category for illegal drugs.

Incarceration started to climb at a slow but steady pace, through the 80's and 90's when the Ronald Reagan Administration began to lead America. From 1980 to 1997 the incarceration rate spiked from 50,000 to 400,000. It was soon after Ronald Regan took office in 1981 the First Lady Nancy Reagan began the anti-drug campaign "Just Say No". Despite the evidence of effectiveness, the DARE program began to grow fast being added to curriculum's in schools across the United States. The founder of the program; Police Chief Daryl Gates believed "casual drug users should be taken out and shot", a statement made by him in an interview during the launching of his program. Although in 1985 a proportion of American's were polled and asked if they thought drug abuse was the #1 problem in the nation, the results were only 2-6% of the people polled believed drugs were the leading problem America faced at the time. The policies only got tougher and tougher as the Clinton and then Bush Administrations took office during the 90's. Offenders were receiving longer sentences for non-violent drug offenses as the prisons were filling up fast. Further, the majority of inmates were and still are forced to accept plea bargains, they plead guilty to an offense that is lesser than what they were charged with, perhaps even one they did not commit. This is a way for the court system to avoid trials which are very costly, therefore they will offer a plea bargain. Most of the time if a case is taken to trial the offender loses and is given much more time than if they would have taken a plea bargain.

The "War on Drugs" started in the early 70's four decades later has back fired and now America is finding itself with over populated prisons, more addicts coming in and out of prison with no treatment, families struggling to make ends meet; because one parent is incarcerated. We are truly backed up against the wall. Prison reform is on the rise however it is a long lengthy process to reverse laws and get a grip on this mass incarceration dilemma. When our loved ones, whether a son, daughter, husband, wife, significant other, or any role they play are incarcerated we too are "Locked Up" with them. Often when someone has a baby you hear "you just have to learn to be a parent, an instruction book does not come with it". It holds true to the incarceration of a loved one, there are many situations, emotions, financial, spiritual, the list goes on, of how we are affected when our LO gets locked up. For some of us it is the first time, others we have seen it over and over. Regardless of what your experience is with incarceration, it is a struggle, something no-one understands unless they too have endured it too. Often we hide it, because of fear people will reject us, they won't understand, or may attach a stigma to us because of the choices of our LO. Therefore, we hold it in and try to deal with it on our own, which in turn can cause a person to grow very tired and weary during the process. My hope for you is this book will not only give you a better understanding of what to expect but will also give you a glimpse into the lives of other inmates and their loved ones, how they are able to cope with "Being Locked Up". From the perspective of Both Sides of the Wire.

Table of Contents

Chapter 1
November 21

"Locked Up" From Both Sides of the Wire was actually in the making for 32 years and I did not realize it, my son's dad was arrested on his first felony back in 1987. We were two teens 18 & 23 our son only 3 years old, his dad about to receive his first charge for possession of methamphetamine. Back in the 80's it wasn't like it is now, meth was considered a new and very dangerous drug. He was only carrying a small amount but it didn't matter we knew he was facing a hefty penalty. He was waiting to enter into the criminal justice system for the first of many offenses to follow, yes bad choices, drugs, being young and wanting to live the street life. At only 21 years old he chose to begin committing crimes to get his drugs, sacrificing his freedom because of his fast growing addiction.

This book is not about addiction, however you will read story after story of individuals that have become addicted and overcame, or sadly some don't escape the horrible disease. Most likely we all have a loved one we have lost to drugs either through the streets, incarceration, or even death. My journey with an incarcerated loved one began many years ago, maybe yours did too, or maybe this is your first time to experience this. Regardless it is not easy, actually I looked up the top 10 stressors adults & children face in America today. According to Blue Cross Blue Shield survey serving time in prison was the #4 cause for adults, and for children #8 a jail sentence of a parent for at least one year or more. I don't think people really realize how stressful it is to have our loved ones locked up until they have experienced it. Even then we don't realize the toll it takes on us, we are in the "free world" but as soon as our LO's are arrested we aren't free either. Those who never experience it; don't understand the pain and suffering we endure from their incarceration. We really shouldn't expect them too either. You can read my book "3 Decades", it tells the whole story of our lives from the first arrest and the 30 years "3 Decades" to follow. How we have made it through, how we learned to cope, through our story we help others gain hope we can and will get through this.

I am going to jump forward a little bit, 3o years to be exact. November 21, 2013 a date no matter what year it is I will never forget. I got the worst call of my life, my son had been arrested on federal charges of conspiracy, taken into federal custody, by U.S. Marshals, Drug Enforcement Agency (DEA), as well as local and state police. Two days prior to my sons arrest his dad was released on what would have been his last prison bid of being in and out for 30 years.

When a federal inmate is taken into custody there is a pre-bond hearing set to decide if the inmate will be released until sentencing court or rather held in federal custody. My son's pre-bond hearing had been set we were waiting in anticipation that he would be released until his sentencing day; which can take up to 3 years. Unlike state charges where you can bond someone out of jail, with federal charges you either are granted or not, pre-bond; if granted you are released until sentencing court if not you stay in county jail until then. Several members of our family went to the hearing, I was unexpectedly put on the witness stand and asked several questions that were geared to testify against my son, yes the federal government is allowed to do this. The way they were describing my son he was being portrayed as a hard core criminal, although his charges were all non-violent. My son had been arrested about 10 days prior to court so things were still fresh and life was horrific, it seemed like the longest week and ½ of my life.

Finally, the day had come for pre-bond court a day that all seems like a blur to me now. I was instructed by a federal agent to take the stand and not make any eye contact or gestures of any kind to my son. With him only about ten feet away from me, his head down, his skin as white as a ghost, he looked as if he hadn't slept much, he was already showing the physical effects of jail and it had only been 10 days. On the stand being asked questions I had no answer's to, my legs shaking, my voice cracking, I couldn't believe what was happening. All I knew was my son and his two very best friends were sitting in a federal court room about to be given their possible sentence by the judge. My son and two other men I had watched grow up for the past 17 years, they are like family to us. I was witnessing before my eyes their lives about to change drastically in an instant.

Devastation could not even come close to how sad I felt inside my heart, especially when the judge denied pre-bond and read his possible sentence of 25 years to life. I didn't understand at that time how minimum mandatory laws worked. How could they sentence someone for a non-violent crime to 25-life was all I could think of. They were charging him with crimes that went on in states he had never been to or known about. When anyone within the same case are involved in crimes, everyone can be charged with all of it.

I managed to make it back to my seat after being interrogated by the prosecuting attorney, my son and his two co-defendants were asked to stand up. All three shackled at the feet and cuffed at the hands stood up and faced the judge. The judge read my son's charges and possible sentence of 25-life, and I remember sitting there in total shock not even being able to process the fact my son may spend the rest of his life in prison. For the first time in his 28 years of life I could not help him, I couldn't save him from this. Not this time, he was in the custody of federal corrections, they owned him now. With my husband, and family by my side all I can remember is running out of the court room, I felt like I wanted to pass out. All I knew was I had to get out of there, I literally felt like I was gasping for air. I had gone through some very stressful times throughout my life, but this by far was the worst. My body was in true shock, I got into my car as we drove home all I can remember is I couldn't move. My body felt locked, my mind blank, all I could do was stare, I hadn't even cried yet. It just wasn't sinking in; I couldn't process this yet. The drive from the court house back home was a little over an hour, it seemed like it took days to get back. I felt the way you do after a funeral of someone close but even worse, wiped out, mentally drained. It is very hard to explain although I am sure most of you understand.

When I made it back home, the first person I tried to reach was my son's dad. He had only been out of prison himself for 12 days. Miraculously I was able to find him pretty quick, usually it could take days. When he called me to find out what was up, the first thing I said was "they got him, he is gone", he said back "what do you mean he is gone, is he ok, what are you talking about". I told him how court went and that he was facing a lifetime sentence. Although his dad was in and out of prison most of his life he loved our son and our son loved him. He wanted to be a dad to him but addiction and incarceration stole his life instead. I know he was responsible for his own actions, however he was an addict that was never treated, a product of being institutionalized. He had gone through several small prison terms 2-4 years and 2 longer sentences the first one 7 years flat and another 9 years flat. I tell you this to give you an idea of how long we had been dealing with incarceration. He was hurt, for the first time in many years I truly could hear the remorse and regret in his voice, he blamed himself for not being there for him all those years. I told him he couldn't think about that now, its history but I did know we needed him now to step up and help get through this. He promised me (which he had done 1000's of times before) he would be there for our son this time; he knew he needed him now more than ever. I believed him one more time, because at that point I was holding onto anything or anyone that could help us. Who better than his own dad is what I thought.

My son in county jail with the worst conditions anyone could imagine waited 2 years to go to sentencing court. I would visit him every week and hear of the horrible conditions of the jail, no recreation time for the inmates, sewer running into his housing area, being put in segregation because there were no other available beds, developing medical conditions due to the filthy jail he was housed in. I filed numerous complaints with jail standards in which the jail was found out of compliance and ordered to fix the problems. I was basically watching my son die, inside and out and it was killing me too. Not only did I develop high blood pressure, I gained 30 lbs., started taking anti-depressants, the feelings of hopelessness would not go away. I couldn't talk of his arrest without crying, I couldn't sleep, didn't want to do much, it was hard to function on a daily basis. Every day seemed to drag on, we would wait for the phone to ring with any news on his case. My husband and God were my saving grace, also my family they helped me each day to become stronger in order to endure the pain I felt. Knowing his fiancé was waiting for him and her dedication to visit him every week has not only given him hope, but also brought comfort to our family.

I was visiting my son for our weekly 20 minutes, I looked so forward to those short visits, even though they were so difficult. I had to arrive at the jail 30 minutes before his scheduled visit, I would watch the other families as I waited. I had seen these two ladies the past few weeks before visitation in the waiting room. They would be in the waiting room the first few minutes I arrived and then go in the back with someone from jail administration. I knew they were not there to visit but wasn't sure what else they could be there every week for. I remember thinking on the way to the visit that day if I saw those ladies I was going to ask them why they came to the jail, what was it they were there to do. Sure enough I arrived for my weekly visit and there they were both ladies with such warm smiles on their faces. There was just something about these women that were different than most people you met. You know when you meet certain individuals and you get a warm feeling about them? That is how I felt just hearing them talk, so I decided to approach them. I began to tell this woman my story in a nutshell, she immediately asked me if I would be interested in coming in sometime to share with the maximum security women housed in that jail. I knew right away this was something I had wanted to do for years although God waited until he knew I needed it as much as the inmates did. I agreed to share my story, this is when I began to learn how to live with the struggle of my son's incarceration. I was asked to come back and be a part of the Overcomers Program they were teaching each week, I was honored and so excited to do that. For the next year and a half every Wednesday morning I would go to the jail and work with those two ladies. I still continue to do prison ministry with them when we travel back to our home state. Those two women I met that day became very dear friends over the next couple of years. It is truly amazing to see God put people in your life that were meant to be there, that is how I feel about them. Not only was it a blessing to them but also to me to be able go inside and work with inmates on a regular basis. It was a very short time after I started going into the county jail I was asked if my husband would want to come into a state prison for men and work the Overcomers Program (A Christ centered program that helps people learn to live with their past, present, and future addictions and vises they face. It is used mostly in the prison system as a way to help inmates learn to heal, forgive, and most of all lean on God for understanding. My husband had not experienced much with incarceration, only my son's encounter. He agreed to come and check it out, instantly after our first visit to share with the men, my husband was hooked, he knew God had sent us to minister to these men and women on a weekly basis. They just wanted to be heard, just wanted someone to listen to them, to let them know someone cared. I will never forget we were meeting with the men for our weekly class and one of the guys said something that really stuck with me. It was around Christmas time, and that is a hard time for both inmates and their LO's as it is. One of the men said "you know we have treats right now, groups coming in to minister to us, bringing us cookies and that is real nice, but it is nothing like knowing that someone came in because they truly cared, most of the time we feel as though we are forgotten by our family and friends". He was basically thanking us just for caring, something I would think comes natural but not in their eyes.

I started to begin to learn how to cope with the reality that my son was locked up, although I never could accept that he would be sentenced to 25-life. That was something that I never would accept, because I knew God would see us through no matter what happened. I've kept my faith, prayed, and believed God would work it out for the best and according to his will. I have good days, and still have many bad ones too. Most often the bad days are because of something he is having to go through. For example, the prison being on lock down which means the inmates are restricted from things like making phone calls, purchasing commissary, getting to go out for recreation (rec), and any other thing they consider a privilege for an inmate. When my son is hurting is when I am hurting, when he is o.k. I can cope much better with his incarceration.

Shortly after my son was arrested in 2013, I started a Facebook page for Incarcerated Loved Ones, and starting sharing positive encouragement for other loved ones. Over the past two years I have watched family members lean on our page for hope, understanding, and mostly a group of people that understand each-others struggle. So often when you have a loved one locked up people who don't have the experience with incarceration tend to judge the situation. I have seen countless families and friends severed due to the incarceration of a LO.

There are people hurting everywhere that don't know where to turn that have loved ones locked up. God put it on my heart to lead the Facebook page, since I have started a ministry Inmate Sharing. Inmate Sharing is a ministry that communicates with inmates and their families through correspondence. I also decided to compile the many letters, poems, stories, art, and other pieces sent in by inmates and their loved ones. I wanted to share "real life" stuff with you all in hopes you can learn to cope, deal with, leave with hope that this too shall pass. So many face the dilemma of incarceration alone, they have no idea where to turn. God put it on my heart to help others by bringing hope, love, and most of all his word, which has grown and continues to grow. I encourage you to sit back and read what others have to say and find ways to connect it to your own situation. Together we can and will get through this.

If you or a LO of yours would like to submit writings to us for future publication send to our address at:

Inmate Sharing, P.O. 352 Beverly, WV. 26241.

Inmatesharing@gmail.com

Please include a statement giving Inmate Sharing permission to publish any and all writings or art sent to us by you. This is a great way to be heard from behind the wire.

Chapter 2
Locked Up

We would have to agree this is an epidemic, one that affects roughly 1 in every 9 people. An estimated 36 million are affected by having an incarcerated loved one. That is a lot of people that deal with the everyday life of having a Loved One locked up in jail or prison. The numbers are growing by the day for LO's experiencing the loss of a loved one through incarceration. Not only do families and friends suffer from the pain of having an incarcerated LO but also the shame, guilt, anger, fear, hurt, confused, the list goes on and on of emotions that arise. Maybe it was a father that got arrested, the one who brought in the paycheck or part of the pay check, this leaves a family financially strapped. It could have been a mother that loses her children because there is no-one to care for them. What about a son or daughter that one day is fine the next hooked on drugs and headed to prison? There are so many situations involved with our experiences of being either an inmate or a loved one of an offender. Both are stressful, what was once one way is now the unknown. I always called it the "unknown" when a loved one got locked up, because so many different situations will come up when our LO is locked up.

With the growing number of people getting locked up each year families are experiencing more and more cases of incarceration. Some have many years of living with the incarceration of loved one, whereas others it is their first time. Regardless of which category you fall in there is still that initial shock of what the first reaction was when you found out. The dreaded call that we have all encountered, the initial arrest. Most often referred to as being "locked up". What does it mean to be locked up? What should we expect? How do we go about getting information? There are so many questions we have when our LO calls and tells us they have been taken into custody, maybe what are they being charged with, how much time will they get? The list just seems to go on and on. Included are the actual comments given by loved ones of inmates when interviewed for this book.

What was your first reaction when you got the call your LO had been arrested, and how was your experience trying find out the charges and/or bond information?

P 1: "I fell apart. totally fell apart. Was I surprised? No. But you are never prepared for those words, they have your son. I had many who loved him that got all the info. for me so I didn't have to. I had given my son to God months earlier, because there was nothing more as a Mother that I could do to stop him from doing what he was doing or to protect him, but I knew God could. Though it broke my heart, I knew that God was working in his life. And now when I start despairing, worrying or crying about him, I have to remember I put my faith and trust in God to save my son. So, that is how I responded, how I deal with it. I just have to keep remembering that I gave him to God. Peace".

P2: "Well, I was completely devastated, felt like I couldn't breathe. I knew it was coming but wasn't ready to accept it at all. I honestly think I had a nervous breakdown, it's the worst feeling in this world is knowing you can't protect or save your child from this cruel world...I felt like a failure".

P3: "I was waking up by my father saying your daughter is on the news and from there it was downhill I fell apart".

P4: "Fell apart got very depress was so angry a sad at same time".

P5: "It was very scary. I had a three-month old breastfeeding baby and I didn't know where to start considering it's was in our neighboring country. The news hit the media and I lost my friends, neighbors, family and the community condemned us. The police roughed us with house search. It was really tough but I trusted God and he remained faithful. I managed to travel and hire lawyers for him and after years' judgment was made and was sentenced to prison. We shall appeal. It's been a journey but God remains God and is faithful forever. He has been my source of strength with my three children. I have a testimony He is able because He has done it for me. My breastfeeding baby will be eleven in September. He is in Grade 6. Those starting the journey, hold on to God and let's all remain strong. He is faithful to take us to the end for them that trust in Him, He renews their strength. We shall not lose faith. Shalom and God bless you all".

P6: "I was present when it happened. My LO was in a drinking and driving accident. I was on the scene with our 8-month old daughter. I'm still stunned how calm I was, I think it was because I had her in my arms too and didn't want my baby to get more scared then she already was. My husband also was in the accident with a woman I found out later he was having an affair with. Because I chose to forgive him and stay with him during his incarceration. I lost a lot of friends and some family because I chose to stay with my husband but I don't care. I know he was using drugs pretty hard and drinking on top of it. He made a huge mistake and now we are facing the consequences together because of it.

P7: "I still don't think I really know how to feel I truly think I'm still in shock. It has only been 2 months but I still cry every day and every night too. I never imagined a loved one getting locked up could have such an impact on the family too".

P8: "I was totally in shock, not because I did not expect it, but because I work for an attorney and we are well known in the courts. I attend meetings with the city officials that work with the criminal justice system, as well as the mayor. I was so worried because I knew they would find out immediately after my husband was arrested, what would I tell them, I didn't know how I could face anyone. Everyone at my kid's school would find out, since my husband's crime was white collar federal crimes we lived a lavish life, people including myself didn't know my husband was committing the crimes, so it was a shock. His dad is a pastor of a church, his mom a school teacher, it was very embarrassing for all of us, especially because we lived in a town of only 10k people so we are very well known. Then there was also the fear of how they would treat my husband there, if they would hurt him, I had no idea what jail was really like. I found a lot of strength from trusting in God and getting on the Incarcerated Group Page on Facebook, it has been such a help. It has made me really realize I am not alone and there are people out here that truly understand and care".

P9: "The jail my son was booked into had a phone number but they did not answer no matter how long I let it ring. I was forced to call a lawyer and have him handle everything for me, not everyone is able to do that, but I recommend even if you have to borrow the money get a lawyer it makes a world of difference. A lawyer can find out the answers to so many questions you will have. If you can't afford a lawyer, then stay on the court appointed one for answers to questions that will arise. Most of the time if you don't ask them they won't tell you the things you need to know'.

P10: "Actually the jail was very helpful when I called to find out the charges and bond for my daughter. I told the lady I had never experienced this before and could she please help me. She walked me through what I needed to know and I was able to get some answers as to what to do next. The bond amount was too high so we couldn't afford get my daughter out but had the jail staff not been so helpful I wouldn't have known what to do".

P11: "All I can say is unfortunately I have experienced having to contact the jail to find out what the bond and charges are for a loved one. The most important thing to remember is they are our loved ones, so stay persistent on calling and asking questions until the information needed is obtained".

P12: "I have to say when I found out my wife got arrested I was not only shocked but very scared. I never experienced anyone I knew going to jail especially my wife, it felt like I was in a horror stories for the first several days. I couldn't tell anyone else until well they just found out through talk around town, I felt so ashamed of the fact my wife had been using and selling drugs for several months and I had no clue. Not only did I have no clue, but I allowed the confidential informant on her case come into our home over and over, thinking she was a friend of my wife, to find out later she set her up".

P13: "Sounds very harsh but I thought well I told you so. My grandson had been running around with the wrong crowd for a couple years, I watched him go downhill fast. I kept telling him if he didn't change his friends and most of all his life he would end up in prison. He chose not to so I chose to not hold on to guilt about the situation. He was already on probation so I didn't even try to bond him out because I knew once he reported the next month, they would ask had he been arrested within last month, as they do every time he reports. When he tells them yes they will arrest him on the spot anyway for violation of his probation, so I didn't waste the money to bond him out for only a couple weeks".

What was the hardest thing to get used to after your LO got locked up?

P1: "The hardest thing to get used to was not being able to just pick up the phone and call or text my son when I wanted to. It took a long time to realize I couldn't just call him, I still have his # programed in my phone with his name and it's not even his number anymore it's been 3 years. I ask myself all the time do we ever really get used to this? I don't think so but I do think we can stay strong and make it through for them".

P2: "Mine has been getting use to not seeing him, or hearing him say mom I'm starving what's for supper, or mom I love you to the moon & back basically everything it was like my whole life stopped when he got locked up".

P3: "The alone feeling every night you crawl in bed. When you were used to them being there and now the pillow is empty night after night that has been really hard for me".

P4: "Not having him help and watch the kids grow. Now I'm really struggling financially to make ends meet since the state only helps with the kid's health insurance and some food. He was the bread winner and now that he is gone it makes it really tough to make it".

P5: "I would truly have to say the hardest part of him not being here is the income, I know that sounds so cold blooded, but my boyfriend was so strung out and abusive life was really bad for a couple years before he got locked up. It is like I don't even remember the real man I fell in love with but I know he is in there. He has been gone 5 months now and it is hard to manage the bills alone, he always brought money in to the house to help. I just hope he gets the help he needs and can stay off the drugs that is my biggest wish".

P6: "I think I would have to say the thing I miss the most is hearing him playing with the kids, my husband is a great dad which makes this so hard. It is hard for me, but to see your kids cry for their dad everyday even after 9 months is even harder".

P7: "I miss everything about my old man that could even be said, most of all I just miss him. He is my best friend, we were together 24/7 now he is gone, it's very lonely. The group page has really helped me get encouragement and meet people I know truly care.

P8: "We worked together so I miss getting up early drinking coffee together and riding to work with each other. That was always our time of the days we would talk and laugh. I am so lost without him, I have found a church I like I go there for friends and the support group on Facebook has truly been a God Sent to me"!

P9: "I am not going to sugar coat it I miss the SEX most of all"!

P10: "I miss the time we spent together, me, my husband, and out 3 kids. Even though we don't have much, we had each other, now that he is gone it makes me feel more alone every day".

P11: "I miss our little family, I had just got married and had a baby the year before he got locked up, he has been gone 4 years now, it seems like we are becoming two totally different people. The thought of us growing apart scares me but I also have to say him being 700 miles away doesn't help either I only get to visit 1 time a year for 2 hours. Makes it very hard on our family, especially when your family and friends tell you to just leave him finally, my heart says no but I mind tells me yes. It's hard" ...

P12: "I miss us cooking together we loved to spend evenings in the kitchen with each other. He would help me cook, set the table, then we would always eat together. It is very lonely sitting at our table alone looking at the chair he always sat in empty".

P13: "The hardest thing to get used to when my son got locked up was him not being there for holidays. My son was always there for all holidays; we would spend the day with the whole family. It took at least 2 years to realize it's just another day, a day closer to him coming home. I don't look at holidays the same anymore not that I look at them as a bad thing now I just think if we keep our faith in God every day of the year why should I get so depressed because it's a holiday, just the way I am able to deal with it better".

P14: "I would have to say the hardest thing to get used to when my nephew got arrested is when he would get moved from jail to prison, or one unit to another, he always got lost in the system. Sometimes it would take weeks for us to hear from him, that is hard not knowing where your loved one is just having to wait day after day. The old way of inmates getting to make one phone call doesn't really hold true anymore. It could take weeks for an inmate to figure out a way to make a call home, this is why it is very important to do inmate searches, call facilities, etc. whatever it takes to locate your LO".

P15: "The hardest part to get used to when my husband got locked up was telling the kids everyday where their daddy is. We have a 3 & 4 year-old so they don't understand why daddy is gone. I just reassure them every day he will be back soon".

When your LO got arrested who was the first person you called and why?

P1: "Unfortunately, when my son got arrested I had been through this so much with his dad over the past 3 Decades I knew right away to call the facility he was in to find out about bond, although it was federal and they don't set a bond. I didn't know this at the time because I had only dealt with state departments over the years. Federal is much different, they don't issue a bond, rather a few days after the arrest they hold a pre-bond hearing to decide whether to grant bond or not, never for a dollar amount, only for the decision whether they will remain in custody or get out until court, it is at total discretion of the judge".

P2: "I called my boyfriend's mom, I knew he was going to need money and I didn't have any".

P3: "The first person I called when my husband was arrested was his brother, he is an attorney and I knew we would need all the advice we could get and also we would need a lawyer as well".

P4: "I called a bail bondsman, they can find out everything you need to know faster than you can and also find out what bail is. What it will take to get them out, and other various information that was very important".

P5: "I called my son's best friend, I knew he would know more than me and could find out what was going on faster than I could".

P6: "First person I called was a babysitter because I knew I was going to have to drive downtown and get him, the jail he was in was huge and would be a stressful trip waiting for his release. It could take hours, last time he got arrested I waited 11 hours after bond was posted for them to release him. Just make sure you are aware of that, bring snacks, or other things you may need if you have to wait a long time".

P7: "This wasn't our first time so I called our attorney they actually have a bond company within their law firm so it makes it easier to get information".

P8: "I called my husband's boss to make up an excuse of why he wouldn't be at work, trying to save him from his job. Although he lost it anyway right when this happened I wasn't thinking of the time he would have to serve".

P9: "The first person I called was the jail to find out what his charges and bond were, of course they didn't know so they told me he would be arraigned in the morning. I called back in the morning and found out what the charge and bond was then called a bail bondsman. I should have just called the bondsman and let him handle that".

P10: "I called my best friend after I found out what he was in jail for and just cried and cried to her. I just needed someone to talk to it was all so scary and new to me. I knew with the charges he was facing it wasn't going to be good, I had never felt this much despair in all my life".

P11: "My first call after I found out my husband was arrested was the pastor of our church. I asked him if he could please pray not only for my husband but also me and the kids. Prayer is what gets me through each and every day he is gone from us. It has definitely helped my faith to grow for sure".

What did you notice first that changed about your loved one after they got locked up?

P1: "My son has so much more patience now waiting for things to happen that had to be so hard to learn from a county jail cell. Waiting to go court for 23 months he sat and waited he learned how to take life as it comes".

P2: "Their attitude, how they talk and act or try to act hard core. But in reality they were crying just like I was when I would leave visit or start to hang up the phone. My daughter became withdrawn, while my youngest got gang affiliated, my oldest now has an attitude I'm going to get you before you get me mentality".

P3: "Actually, his handwriting and spelling improved a lot. He is dyslexic but got himself a dictionary and finally I could decipher letters when he writes to me".

P4: "Him realizing who actually loves and cares about him and realizing his "friends" really aren't friends!! This is the biggest thing we have both learned since he got locked up.

P5: "His faith in God has definitely grown more than anything! He was going so fast with drugs and street life before he got locked up I don't think he would have ever seen it. He probably would have got killed or died some way, he knows that so I would have to say his relationship with God has changed drastically.

P6: "I believe God is working in my son's life. I just finally gave it all to God, because I could see that road he was on. Now, he's a completely different person, and I believe it is God working in his life. My son looked so broke when I first saw him this time in there, and someone reminded me to give him to God, that he was shaping him into the man he meant for him to be. Thank you God. I truly believe I have my son back, even though he is still locked up".

P7: "My honey is way more jealous and worries about me so much more when he's inside. I suppose it's because he's not here to protect me and he's afraid I'll get taken advantage of or hurt".

P8: "His whole demeanor, his one and only real child was born 10 days after he left the county jail going to prison. The mom of his child just decided it was best for him not to see her until he gets out well she's fixing to be 6. Then he had to realize all his friends were not true friends, he had to learn how to handle losing his dad, aunt, and grandma all within 1 year. But, by the grace of God he is seeing that he is stronger and keeping his faith in God has made him realize who he can trust. He's learned so many things since he has started his prison sentence".

P9: "I am so happy that my son's girlfriend takes his daughter to see him. She has decided that even if they don't make it as a couple when he gets released, he will be a part of his little girl's life. That makes me very happy. But the funny thing is, my son has become the strong one, the one who uplifts all of us in his letters. He has accepted that he made those choices and he now has to pay for them. He also for the first time, accepted that if it wasn't for God, he would not even be here to write us, be a part of his daughter's life, or just be alive. This is the son I remember so long ago. I thank God every day for what he is doing in his life. When I start worrying, I remind myself, I gave it to God, the best thing a parent can do. Faith keeps me knowing all is in the hands of God, and it will all be alright. I believe his daughter was a wakeup call for both him and his girlfriend. His GF has turned her life completely around. And now for the first time ever, my son will get out and his mate will be clean and leading a life he has really always wanted. God works in very mysterious ways. My son has always had "so called friends" waiting on him with a bowl of Meth as a welcome home, dude. That has really rubbed me the wrong way. This time, most all his real friends are clean and sober, leading productive lives or they have died from the life style. I believe my son is coming home as a man who is truly ready to live his life for God".

P10: "The thing I noticed that has changed about my son the most while he has been locked up is he is so antisocial now. When I go visit him he always wants to sit in the back of the room where the wall is behind him. He says once you have been locked up you learn to look on all sides of your being at all times, even when you sleep you have to be on the lookout".

How have you been treated differently by others due to the incarceration of your Loved One?

P1: "Some shunned me or gossiped about me or told me how stupid I was for waiting for him. Others I gained respect from for having no shame about this, for being adamant in keeping my promise not to abandon him (which I have not) and for my sincere participation in Texas prison reform".

P2: "I would have to say I am not really treated different, but we lived in a town since my son was only 4, he grew up there, a basketball star for the high school team, class clown, very popular and loved by so many. When he got arrested I heard so many rumors others had been told about my son's case that were totally off and not true. It doesn't bother me what others think at all because my son is my son, but I do pick and choose who knows about our situation not because of being talked about but because it is simply none of their business. I have learned through all of this we don't have to share everything with people".

P3: "The people I've met on Facebook, mostly through the prison support groups, were the most amazing support system anyone could have wished for during this time of having my boyfriend locked up and cancer. I am so blessed and I am so grateful for each of you. God bless you all."

P4: "The only people that know about my husband being incarcerated are my family or very close friends. It is not that I am ashamed of it but my job as a physician requires confidentiality about my personal life. Yes, I am a doctor and my son is in prison, it can happen to any person regardless of their race, occupation, religion, or other ethnic background".

P5: "Everyone has an opinion about the way I've chosen to handle the situation! Some respect me more for the way I am dealing with it, some say I'm doing too much, others say I don't do enough. The most difficult thing is men that call themselves his friend! In one breath it's "send Outlaw my Love" and the next it's "so when can I take you out"! REALLY? My husband is locked up, not dead"!

P6: "Oh yeah my family has disowned me because my husband got arrested again and I told them I was going to wait on him. We have been together for 8 years and this is the 3rd time my husband has caught charges. We have 3 kids and I love him very much, I always tell people you don't understand unless you have walked in my shoes. To walk away from my husband because he got arrested to me would not be right. My husband is on paper for 5 years and they make it impossible to get through it. This time he missed 2 months of probation costs so they revoked him and he will have to do a year in state jail. They see him as a horrible convict and I see him as someone who got caught up in the system that can't get out".

P7: "I lost my car, my job, and almost my kids. The incarceration of my husband was real hard for me and I almost thought I couldn't cope without him. Then when I realized I was about to lose my kids I gave my life to God and am learning how to deal with this in time. So I would say yes I was treated differently by many when my husband got locked up, it is like no one wants to help when you are waiting for your husband that is locked up."

Chapter 3
Until Next Time...

Although we don't understand things most of the time as they are happening, I have learned if we trust in God and watch for his answers he will show us. Sometimes it takes longer than we want to wait, however we must always remember it is in God's timing and will, not our own.

During my son's county jail, the 2 years before court he met a lot of other men in the same predicament as him. He doesn't friend too many people very easy he is the type of guy if he is your friend he is a true one. One out of the three county jails he was in, the one he was in for the longest with the worst conditions, he met a guy name Kevin. Him and Kevin got pretty tight, there were times they were in an 8-man POD just the two of them and other times they were jammed in there 8 men deep. But him and Kevin always managed to keep each other a float. One would encourage the other when life seemed at its worst. They made it through several months together which in turn built a bond between the two of them. I continued to stay in contact with Kevin, I am very grateful to him for the love he showed my son when he needed it most. It meant a lot to me as a mother, Kevin just always seemed to be able bring my son up when he was down. To remind him to keep his mind strong, to exercise; regardless if it meant in a jail cell with 7 other men, to perseveres and always keep his eyes of God. Kevin started writing blogs for our Facebook page and they were such an inspiration to so many loved ones and brought so much information to them, we (Kevin & I) decided to use them to publish. To help others understand some of the things that will come up during their loved one's incarceration, answers to many questions a loved one may have. It is Kevin's hope that as many loved ones of the incarcerated will find the information not only informative but also helpful.

On November 10, 2010 my life changed forever, it was a date that as set in motion, months before hand by events that seemed insignificant, compared to what I believed was the big picture. Sometimes in my case you think you can outsmart the game, but all it takes is one little mistakes that makes the whole house of cards fall.

Prior to November 10th I was in the life hot and heavy. I was just starting to get going, so I thought, and getting my money right. I was running the streets, without a driver's license, pushing drugs, mainly meth and marijuana, but honestly I would sell anything anyone would buy, or that I could get my hands on. That is one thing about drugs they will sell themselves. I honestly thought I had my life together. I had fast money coming in, so I spent my money as fast as I could get it. I would hit the bars every night with all my so called "homeboys", get drunk, shoot pool, and kick back. We knew all of the bar owners, and eventually started selling one of them ice when I would go to his bar frequently. He used to get trashed with us and need to get high to sober up. The bar owner was cool, and I kicked it with this dude a lot, so I wasn't worried that he was on any police-type stuff. What I hadn't considered was maybe the people around him were. I was never just super faded until I got done hustling for the day. Once I hit the bar though, all bets were off. I am not making excuses for anything, but in a lack of judgement, I continued my dope selling. I started selling the bartender meth (ice) as well. I figured if I could go to the bar and hit two "licks" while I was going there anyway, why not, the more sales the better for me so I thought. Seemed simple at the time, but this led to my downfall. I didn't have any business selling to this dude, and I always told my homeboy that I thought he was shady. My logic was that I've already sold to him once, so if he is the police there is nothing I can do about it now. At the time I was 25 years old and no-one could tell me anything. Long story short, this guy calls the Sheriff's Department and asks if they want to make a drug bust? This guy never been in trouble nor had any issues with my partner or I. He just called out the blue and worked it out to make controlled buys from me and my partner. I saw the whole thing play out and still went with it.

This individual named as the CS (Confidential Source) in my discovery made 6 controlled buys from my partner and I. He wore a camera inside a residence that the county stated was managed by my partner and I, and took pictures of the residence, items inside, as well as money, drugs, and firearms, among many other things. The county had enough evidence to move in on us and they did.

November 9, 2010, the day before our arrest I did what I do every day of the week, hustle, and got loaded. I was drunk and I called my partner and said "man their fixing to kick in our door, I know you got to feel it too because you haven't been crashing here, I am about to pack up and get out of here". I told him "I am not staying here anymore". He agreed and we said we would talk in the morning about what we need to do. I had 2 family members in the house at the time, and a chic that came by to get high and kick it with me. It just didn't feel right though, I felt in my gut something was just not right. I told the chic to go home I just didn't feel like company at the time, and I continued to get drunker and drunker on Crown Royal Black and Coke, until I passed out. I had every intention of leaving, but I woke up and was still drunk, I figured I was just tripping, and one more day would not hurt to stay.

It was around 6 a.m. in the morning, the taskforce, served a no-knock entry warrant into the residence. All I could hear was yelling, police! police! The door was being kicked in, one of family members got hit in the process and screamed, they are here, they are here! It was total chaos to say the least. I thought about jumping out the bedroom window, but I didn't want to leave family that I loved in a house full of drugs, guns, and paraphernalia for them to have to deal with. I just laid down in the bed face down with my hands behind my head, I did this because in the bed with me I had a pistol. Another pistol on the night stand, and another gun with a 100 round magazine in the corner floor. I also had a 357 in my dresser drawer, I wanted to make sure I didn't get shot by the SWAT team that was about to kick my bedroom door in. That is exactly what they did, it only took 2 kicks to get through and once they did they hollered commands at me not to move, and that I was under arrest. As two officers restrained me, the others started searching the room, opening the closet and found pounds of marijuana. The officer got the attention of another to show him what he found and they high-fived one another celebrating their find. It was a great moment for them, as I watched my future unravel before my eyes. The deputies dressed me while I was cuffed with a shirt, shorts, and shoes and escorted me to the front yard and into a squad car. I looked around and there were at least 10 cars and two transport vans in the front of the residence. SWAT team officers everywhere with masks, and tactical gear. My heart was pounding inside my chest as the adrenaline pumped through my body. A deputy in a ski mask approached the vehicle I was being contained in and asked "what is the combination of the safe"? I replied "I don't know what you are talking about, and that I needed a lawyer". The officer said back to me "you think you are a gangster riding around my town selling dope". I said "well at least I don't hide behind a mask like you do when I go to work". Our discussion ended quickly, the officer instructed another "take him to the jail". I was actually glad because I was hung over and did not want to deal with hostile police officers at the time.

I was driven to the county jail and put in a cell by myself, with no access to a phone. They wanted to get my partner and I both at the house, but he wasn't there. They locked my aunt in a cell down the hall from me. I could hear someone yelling down the hall "Kevin, I love you" I yelled back "they are putting everything on me, so don't say anything". The jail guards yelled at me to shut up, but I had to make sure she knew what was going on. It got me put into segregation until I was finally bonded out.

I signed my bond papers at the bond hearing company, talked to a lawyer, and weighed my options. They had charged me with not under lbs. but not over 50lbs of marijuana, over 4 but under 200 grams of controlled substance, and possession of stolen firearms, I was hit! I lost a lot of money, drugs, vehicles, and owed my plug (connection). When you get busted the bills keep piling up, and income stops. I could cut my losses and fight my case with a public offender ("pretender") and try to stay out of the way, or I could dig myself out of this hole I put myself in. So I grabbed my shovel, and buried myself.

Until next time, Kevin

"Getting Started"

This post is to help "Loved Ones" LO's of inmates get a hold of their family members, put money on their books, get mail to them, and know how to send care packages. The first month is the hardest because you can't use the money that was sent with you from county, most people you are locked up with are broke, and you and your family members are freaking out because they don't know where you are, haven't had a call because you have no way to make one, this makes you worry, on top of fear of the unknown it's very chaotic time for the inmate and their loved ones too.

Let's get started with find your incarcerated LO because you can't write them or put money on their books until you find them. Once you have found out that your incarcerated LO has caught chain go to the state's corrections website there should be an offender search available for each state. However, if your inmate is a county jail being transferred between county jails it could take up to two weeks, or some cases a month to locate them. Whatever you do don't freak out if you can't find them, they are just what you call "lost in the system while in transit" Once your incarcerated LO makes it to his or her final stop they will find a way to get a hold of you, and most likely have been assigned an inmate number. Once inmates are assigned a number you will be able to locate them a lot sooner regardless of where they are sent. An inmate number is used for everything, from commissary to mail, to visitation so be sure to write it down and keep it in a safe place.

Once you find your LO you're going to want to make contact with them as soon as possible. If they are in county jail and you can get money on their commissary as soon as possible so they can call you, that is the best way. You can call the facility and find out what commissary company is used as well as the phone account. The inmate will figure out other ways by other inmate's cheaper ways to call and send correspondence however that takes some time. There is always the snail mail way to get in contact, and also jPay.com works for most state prisons. If it is a federal facility go to BOP.gov for any information needed. Trust me we want to hear from ya'll as soon as possible too because by now we are tripping from not being able to contact our loved ones. No matter what we say, we are on edge. We don't admit it usually but our biggest fear in prison or jail is being alone and not knowing what's going on. I have seen dudes go months without hearing from anyone. We call mail call stress call where I am, I have seen guys not get up next day and work out, or sit in their bunks all day, be out of there for the day because they didn't get mail again. Mail is SERIOUS here. I have literally seen guys look like they made parole when they hear from someone. So always try to locate your inmate and write to them as often as you can.

Until Next Time, Kevin

"Commissary is necessary"

On the weekend they only feed twice a day in most units now. Not only is food important, but hygiene is important too. You don't want your LO getting beat up because they smell like onions, or even worst BO, because they have no money for deodorant. If you can let your inmate know somehow you put money on their books because a lot of times we are not notified if we have money and won't know. All joking aside commissary seems like a luxury to people who never been locked up, but not having commissary make your time that much harder. We call commissary here the "Walk of Shame" where you go all the way across the unit to the window to find out there is nothing there, waited in line hoping the entire time there is something there to be denied is not a good feeling.

A lot of LO's are super anxious to set up the phone, but you shouldn't stress about this, your incarcerated loved one won't be able to use the phone until they see classifications. Which could also take two to three weeks, this could vary from unit to unit. So remember even though you have set up the phone account and still don't hear from your LO they are not able to use the phone yet is most likely the case.

I hope this entry will not only help you find your LO, but make contact with them and go about sending what they need when and if you can. From our perspective in here mail, phone, store, and visits are essential to an inmate. A simple one-page letter, $20 on their commissary, or a quick phone call means so much in the eyes of an inmate. I know we stress you all out in the world but we just want yall to know all we need is to know we aren't forgotten; it can make all the difference in how we do our time.

Until Next Time, Kevin

"Ol Jody"

"Jody" is a jail term for a guy who is taking your spot with your girl, wife, or baby momma while you're in prison. It's a tough reality that a lot of my fellow convicts go through. I've got a "Jody" at the house right now, laid up with my wife. I can't be mad at her because we weren't together when I got locked up. It still sucks though!

The two hardest ways to do time in prison is with an old lady and without one. It sounds crazy but let me explain. When you have a girl or wife you stress, BIG TIME. The first couple of months is ok, mail is on-time, visits every week, and money is on your books. It's all good, the pattern I have seen is around 18-24 months is when it usually starts "falling off". I only know how to describe it as the "fall off". "Falling Off" is a term that every convict knows as when women fall off while she's riding with you. Your conversations go from "I Love You and just you to "years are just too long to wait". Mail becomes a thing of the past and that's when you start looking for pen pals. Girls or guys that are locked up and lonely too, looking to kill some time with a pen & paper. Nothing wrong with it in our eyes, I wrote 4 different pen pals in the 3 ½ years I been locked up, just not the same though, not the same as someone you know, love, and miss so much.

That brings me to my second point: doing time with no one at your side. I think out of the two options it is the easiest though. At first it was so hard because I had a wife, and it didn't work out, but once I got passed the gut wrenching pain (about a 1 ½ years) it was brutal, my time got a lot easier. The upside down of not stressing over your woman makes time a lot easier to handle. During visitation day I don't wait for visits anymore from my wife and kids, I don't have anyone to call, and now I don't trip on not getting mail. I know none of those things are coming, so I don't wait for them anymore. It's better to not see, hear, or believe the lies, that's what was making my time hard. The down side of not having loved one's support is of course the no support, no visits, no money on books, and no phone calls. My wife and I over the past 3 years has tried to work it out but she has "Sancho" still laid up. Sancho is Jody's Hispanic brother. White guys use the term Jody; Hispanic guys use Sancho. The "Ol Jody" is an issue that affects all races, genders, and sexual preferences. I can't count how many of my homeboys I've had to talk to and calm down because they are tripping about their chicks. Yelling on the phone, writing them hate mail letters. I have seen the hardest core gangster dudes cry like babies over their significant other. Here is my philosophy, if you can't give me any time while I am here then you don't get my time when I get out. That is what I tell myself anyway, I have had girls write me tell me they are going keep it real, because they aren't like all the rest, I have even tried to pimp my pen and pick up a new girl. It just never works out that way.

A relationship started and based on lies, usually doesn't last believe me I have tried it a hundred times.

This is just my opinion, and this is not the case every-one only the vast majority, there are still some "ride or die" women out there, they are just few and far between. They are a blessing, a relationship centered around God are the ones that I see last. Both of you are on the same page, and going in the same direction even though yall are apart, you have a better chance of making it.

A lot of dudes in here may say I am going to buy "Ol Jody" a beer when I get out for paying the bills while I was gone. Sounds good? A pair of lips will tell you anything you want to hear or they want to try and believe especially when they are wearing the same jail jumper as you. The truth be said if your man, baby daddy, husband, whatever he is to you is locked up, just keep it 100% with him. Tell him the truth, it may hurt but it is best for him to be able to move on. It will be better in the long run for everyone involved. I am sure yall do love us, but we are just too locked up. It is very hard to maintain a relationship apart. It just is, covering it up just makes things so much worse. Be honest with each other and pray it works out for the best, they say absence makes the heart grow fonder, but sometimes that is not the case. Sometimes absence begets more absence.

In closing, relationships are a double edge sword that could be your biggest source of comfort, or your hardest. The best advice I can give you homeboys is don't stress, it won't help either way. In fact, it will make your time harder. Focus on doing your time, coming home, and changing your life for the better. Be productive, here is my motto now: I refuse to let anyone make me weaker, including myself. Don't do someone else's time, instead do your own time, be the best "you" can be.

Until Next Time, Kevin

"Don't Believe the Hype"

I finally touched down at my unit after 3 ½ years in county jail waiting for sentencing. "Butt Naked" is what we call this transfer unit, so named because the laws were known to strip you out in a moment's notice. The title of this blog is "Don't Believe the Hype" in this entry I want to dispel the rumors that first timers hear in county and lace you up on what is really going on in the now.

As of December 2015 I have only been naked once by order of good for a search, and that was five minutes off the chain bus. Another rumor is when you get to prison they strip you down and make you go "nuts to the butts" as you go through intake. They used to line you up butt naked with your toes almost touching the guy in front of you which would put your nuts to butts. This is no longer a practice in most units across America. They do line you up heel to toe in rows, and have you strip in each row, but afterwards you put your boxers on as they rotate you through various cages as you go through intake. After your paperwork is signed and you have answered the standard questions you get your head shaved. Yes, this is still in practice so if you have long hair or dreads or anything other than a zero on the clippers kiss it goodbye. Another myth I have heard is the clippers are so hot from cutting a hundred heads, that they burn the scalp. FALSE! The shaving I received was ok I was actually thankful to get a free hair cut after being charged in county, for clippers that were actually hot.

After having your beloved hair chopped off, you are given a shower roll which includes, a small worn out towel, cheap razor, and a motel size bar of soap, and sent to an area labeled S for a shower and shave. It is required to keep a clean shave here at this unit, from what I have heard they are lightening up on letting beards grow due to religious laws.

After our shower and shave session we move on with 4 other offenders, you get issued your dingy whites, if you want clean nice ones you have to pay for them. We then were run through a process like county jail, fingerprints, mug shot, and a housing number. This place use to have you shower "butt naked" with no curtain right under the TV's that is also a thing of the past, now there are curtains blocking the day room. These policies were put into place a few years back which has made the shower shark start to become an extinct animal; a shower shark is when someone tries to watch other men or women shower on the cool. Yes, it happens, sad but true. For us first timers that are told prison will be so much better than county jail, boy where we misinformed it is laid back and the commissary is cheaper is about the only difference I have seen so far. They do feed better here and we can move around so I guess that does make it better in a way.

The first week I arrived here time flew by, I had what is called lay ins basically appointments to get everything taken care of for intake requirements. Which included medical exams, orientation, education assessments, drug assessments and all sort of classes, that was definitely different from county. It is still prison and you have to stay on your P's and Q's at all times.

Once I am classified I will be moved either to another building or another facility, depending on how classification decides to house me. I will be on another unit shortly but in reality who knows what they do and when they do it.

In closing I would like to tell anyone going down for the first time "Don't believe the Hype". Don't believe anything anyone tells you about what prison will be like, especially when they are in the same jail issued clothes you are. Everyone likes to pump stuff up, the only rumors that are true is there is no AC here in Texas prisons, the biscuits are huge, and they do only serve 2 meals on Saturday and Sunday. I am sitting here right now and can vouch for everything I have told you, it is weak here and slow. There is no movement of stuff from the kitchen or anything extra going on, we are just all trying to make parole. I hope you all read and enjoy this blog, I will continue to keep you all posted about my movement from unit to unit, when I make parole from state and are then sent to the FEDS for the remaining of my sentence. I am going to try keep it interesting so you all ride it out with me, thanks for reading. God Bless You All!

Until Next Time, Kevin

"Dead Time"

    Throughout my incarceration I've met a lot of men with the same problems that I myself faced when I first got locked up: dead time. There isn't much to do in a county jail that's productive, and the dead time is the biggest enemy to a men's mind, body, and spirit. Inmates all over the world sit around stressing about their time, their family, their cases, having money on their books, visits, mail. The list goes on and on, we as inmates want something, anything to break the monotony, even if it means something negative or destructive. Stress, boredom, and monotony turn a cell into a boiling pot of convicts just waiting to explode. And a lot of the time we do explode.

    A lot of the time we let the time do us, instead of us doing the time. This is my old jailhouse cliché but basically we have to learn to use our time of incarceration to benefit us, instead of letting our time beat us down, and turn us into something worse than we were when we came in. I've seen men sit back and lay in their bunk all day every day and wonder why nothing is going on with their cases. I've watched 19 and 20 years old kids talk about when they get to prison how they are going to get their heart check, ride with a gang, and get back to hustling on the streets as soon as they make parole. I've heard older convicts talk about how they are going to kill their ole ladies and their boyfriends when they get out. These are mindsets that show weakness in men and women. This is what I refer to as locked up mind frame. Often being locked up makes inmates believe that their situations are someone else fault. That hustling or robbing, stealing, or getting high is "what's up", but when it comes time to pay the consequences it's a different story. That to me is taking advantage of women or weaker individuals, abandoning their kids, and poisoning their communities with drugs are all acceptable, if not applauded. I see it glorified in jail in conversations, tattoos, and drawings. I see it glorified in movies, books, magazines, and music. We as men have believed what the world has told us is ok, and live with it. We have allowed ourselves to be brainwashed by what society has fed us, and we keep asking for more no matter who it hurts.

During my time I have seen a lot of men defeated, angry, lost, and hurting. There is nothing worse than being in jail or prison, alone, and not knowing where you are going. It is a hopeless feeling in your stomach like when you lean back to prop yourself against a wall that isn't there.

So I challenge you to make a declaration of manhood to be the best father, son, husband, leader, and the man of God that you can be, and that God wants you to be. To take responsibility of the life God gave you, and to be good stewards with the things he gives you. You have a purpose and direction that you were created for. The best way to find it is get on your knees and ask God what direction he wants you to go in, then don't just walk in that direction, run in it. We've already given the criminal justice system enough of our time, it's time that we start giving our families, our wives, and our children the time that we so aimlessly given away to frivolous purposes. It's time we take a stand and take the lives back that we were intended to live, and lean our families in that direction with us.

It is time we get busy! You don't have time to waste anymore, because every second that is gone can't be regained. Don't look back at the past. God forgives us all, if we ask, it's that simple all we have to do is ask. Now it's time to move forward. Even if you have a life sentence, you can still shed the incarcerated mind frame. You still have a purpose and responsibility. Get out of that bunk and be what God intended you to be, a MAN!

Until Next Time, Kevin

"Prison Commissary"

Ok, I finally got a copy of the unit I am on commissary list, the pricing is insane, the mark up is really high. This is just the prisons prices; county jail is about double. There is no telling what they mark it up from the wholesaler's price. This is a post to let you know how much they are gouging us. This is how they get away with it: most people in county jail are only there for 3-6 months, maybe a year at max. Most people moved around too quickly to see the long term financial binds that $1 soups, and .10 sweetener put in. When you are in federal custody, it's a different story. I did 3 ½ years in county before coming to prison a few months ago, and let me tell you it is hard to get someone to take care of you for that long, especially when it's no one's fault but your own.

Another way county jails get away with getting down on us is that commissary is considered a privilege. If you get into any trouble in county, prison, or federal prison, they are going put you on commissary restriction (among other restrictions, such as no visitation, phone calls, any contact with the outside other than snail mail) for a certain amount of time, usually increments of 15, 30, 45, days etc. I don't get it, if I tell you that it is a privilege for you to buy drugs from me is that ok? Are these double standards that plague not only our jails and prison, but our society in general? Let me or you do something illegal, and say it is a privilege and see if we get away with it, only the government can do that. I really wish there was a platform to screen this out. This is an ongoing issue that affects both people inside and outside of prison, and is oppression. The government putting their foot on our necks, when we're already down for the count.

Until Next Time, Kevin

"Parole Packet"

The number one worry in prison is making parole, it is a crazy thing how little I see people trying to make parole. "The Young and the Restless" is not going to help anyone make parole! Anyone who has been in prison knows what I am talking about. Change the TV off of Young and Restless if you want to try make parole, you need to be ready to fight! Its serious thing in prison, crazy as it may sound, in fact as I sit at this stainless steel table, it is on the TV right now. My point is this: if you want to make parole, do everything within your power to get it done. This week's entry is about Parole, and what an inmate can try to do to increase the chances of making parole.

The first option which is the easiest option is getting a parole attorney, however the most expensive route to go on an average $1500. What a parole attorney will do is write a parole packet and represent you in a parole interview. The good thing about hiring a parole attorney is you will have no work to do, other than give your attorney the necessary information to fill in a template parole packet. The parole packet will then be sent to the Board of Parole. If you are able to hire an attorney, make sure research is done before hiring an attorney. The downside of hiring a parole attorney is that they aren't guaranteed an interview with the Parole Board before they make your parole decision. If your attorney promises you he/she can, be careful because there are no guarantees in the criminal justice system. Unless there are disputes with your parole packet that would cause the parole board to vote against you, in my opinion an attorney is not required in order to work on your own parole packet.

The second option, and more difficult one is to write your own parole packet, and send it to the Board of Parole yourself, this takes a lot more work, but I think the rewards are worth the labor. Plus, we have nothing but time! I despise that jail cliché but it's true. It also shows the parole board that you took initiative in writing your own packet, also it is a lot cheaper this way. Postage, paper, envelopes, and time is what it takes to write your own parole packet. Here is the thing about the parole board it isn't an assembly of voters, the voter votes and sends it to the next voter (member of the parole board). So there is no actual board or panel that views your case. I still feel like it is important to communicate to the board your remorse, your future plans when you are released and why you should be released. Why not save your family money when you can spend about a week putting this together yourself? I am actually working on mine now I got classified a few months ago and found out I am now parole eligible. It's easy to write your own parole packet, it is about 20-30 pages long but if you need an example Google "How to Write Parole Packets".

In conclusion, there is a limited amount of things we as inmates can do to make parole. The most important thing we can do is keep from getting cases while in the "pen". No tattoo or cigarette is worth losing out on time with your family. Stay focused on coming home and not on the jailhouse politics. Do your time, not someone else's time, I hope this entry was helpful, I felt it was critical information that everyone in prison and their loved ones should know. Keep your head up convicts! As yall know this is just a minor setback to a major come back. Just keep in mind your family needs you!

Until next Time, Kevin

"Nicknames"

Nicknames are a common thing in prison. The majority of people in prison don't want people to know their real names. It's just a common thing, that I think will never die. Some people bring their nicknames from the world, while others get them in prison. Some guys get them in prison, go home, come back to prison, and use the same nickname. It's also not strange to have people with the same nickname. I am in "F" building and there are 3 guys name "Solo" in here.

Sometimes nicknames are given because of the person's physical appearance. I met a "Potato Head" who got this name because he had a large head with a potatoes shape. "Rib Cage" because when he gets high you can see his ribs, when he normally weighs around 220lbs. "Shorty's are name usually because of their stature. A lot of times nicknames start as jabs or minor insults that eventually stick. My homeboy "Little Foot" got his name because he has a clubbed foot, and has one smaller foot and leg. In the penitentiary you have to have thick skin and don't get into your feelings, or wear your emotions on your sleeves. They are really terms of endearment in a testosterone fueled environment.

Some convicts get their names because they resemble a celebrity. My cellie is called "Bieber" for having some of Justin Bieber similarities, I think he only has a minimal resemblance, at best, but it stuck. Another homeboy Bird (childhood nickname) cellie we called "Clint

Eastwood". "Scarface" is a pretty common one, Bigg Head, and the list goes on.

Sometimes nickname start just because you don't know someone names, so you just start calling them what comes to mind. Someone will say "who" you will say "old boy in bunk 36", everyone laughs and a nickname is born, it's that easy. Everyone here calls me "Bags" because my knuckles say Body Bags and now I hear it every day like it's the name my mom gave me. There is Ace, because he is an Ace in the Hole, can always depend on him. I've been locked up with "White Mike", "Shaggy", "Soundman", "Twisted", "Creature", "Suzuki", and all kinds of other names given to us convicts. Here there is a plethora of characters with a variety of nicknames. If you are a people watcher, there is no end of entertainment in prison. If you spend enough time here you get a nickname, whether you want to or not. I hope this has given you some insight and entertainment on how we get our nicknames in prison.

Until Next Time, Kevin AKA BAG$

"Vocational Programs"

Most prisons offer some type of vocational programs, that convicts can apply to take to further their education that will help them in the "free world". I just recently applied to take an auto body class. Something that should be considered before applying for a vocational class, once approved the inmate will be moved to the unit that offers the program. It has been told to me in orientation that if our people choose to pre-pay for the vocational class or college course that you will be on an ID unit within two weeks. Otherwise it could take a while to get into a vocation of choice. Paying for a class off of commissary will do the same thing as your people paying for it. This is a good thing to get to an ID unit where you can get a fan, hot pot, and radio, without getting G4'd (sent to medium custody). That's what everyone here is trying to do get off of these 2 year transfer units and get to an ID unit and start doing some real time.

To apply for programs, write a request to whoever is over the education programs and request a program of choice. They will send you the form with instructions the form will require some personal information, and will ask if you plan to get a degree or certificate, and the requirements needed for each degree offered. You must have your GED to qualify for any of the courses and you have to have a certain score on your test given at the beginning of the process.

The form usually asks to select two programs of choice they range from culinary arts, welding, computer repair, drafting, masonry, and many more. There is also a way to get in quicker if you are willing to pay for the courses selected. There is a 3rd way to try get into programs which is the hardest but I have seen guys get in its called "The Hazelwood Benefits" this is for some inmates that qualify because of time spent in the armed services.

I believe in us convicts getting an education so when we get back into the free world we have something other than "Hustlin" to work with. This is a way we can maximize our lives in a legal way, don't get down if it takes a while to get approved for programs it is a process just like the rest of the processes we go through in here. Proverbs 8:11 tells us "for wisdom is better than rubrics, and all the things one may desire cannot be compared". Throughout the Bible God command, us to seek knowledge. I hope this helps you in your journey with being in prison, next week I will write about how to receive "Time Cuts", I know there are so many rumors about "time cuts" I am going to fill you in and let you know the truth.

Until Next Time, Kevin

"Time Cuts"

I finally received the information and application for what is formally known as commutation of sentence. It is available in the state you reside in as part of the Administration Code, you can go to the law library and look it up for yourself if you are locked up. If you're a loved one trying to figure it out, you can look it up on the internet. One of the things I hate the most is penitentiary rumors about new laws that are fixing to get passed, for instance the 35% AGG (aggravated) time in Texas Prisons, or 65% in the feds, these are time reductions that can be looked up by one's self. Most states you can go online and request an "application for commutation of sentence to the Board of Pardons and Parole, they should have the paperwork available, if you don't have anyone that can obtain that paperwork for you, there is always the option to write the state parole office and request it. Once the application is completed send it to the parole board for your state, they will vote to send the request to the Governor, not to say it is impossible although the odds are slim. I never want to discourage anyone from trying, I just want to inform you before you get your hopes up for a time cut.

Things are moving in a better direction for us convicts as far as getting out of prison sooner than we thought originally. Most states the prisons are full and they are granting parole a lot faster than in the past. I see people here who genuinely should not be in prison and only signed for time because they were bullied by the prosecutors, DA, and even their own lawyers. Pushed into hefty sentences because if they didn't sign a plea bargain they could be hammered with life sentences. I never wanted to sign for 30 years but my prosecutor told my lawyer that if I didn't sign she would give me a life sentence. How can she sentence me when I would have been tried by a jury? Sounds to me like the government is playing with an already stacked deck, we are victims of this money machine that takes money from tax payers to house us, from our family member that pay huge fees to give us commissary, and from us when we get out on parole. Once you add it all up and put the pieces together it seems like we are all being hustled. Most of us are hustlers in the "free world" and know when we see it. It's crazy how the government pimps its own people for a dollar. There is so many of us that feel oppressed, and we are sick and tired of it! Thanks again for your time and I hope this has been good information for someone out there.

Until Next Time, Kevin

"Lockdown"

For those of you who are new to this prison thing, each unit does a routine lock down twice a year. We just came off of ours, it lasted 9 days. Day 1 they called us out for work at 4:30 a.m. as usual for laundry per usual on Monday mornings. When we got to laundry they sent us back to our dorm, because nobody was in the laundry room to supervise us. We thought that was odd and started speculating among each other about a lock down, we had heard for the past 3 months it was coming. Once we got back to our dorm we waited about 15 minutes and they call us all back out. We get back to laundry and our laundry boss is there, so we think everything might be on the up and up. Then the CO (correctional officer) comes in and jumps down our laundry boss throat about us being down there, and she said she didn't know. So none the less, we knew what time it was, time to go back to our dorm again. Around 6:00 a.m. the guards came in our dorm and laid down the ground rules. You can't get off your bunk unless it is to use the bathroom. The showers were closed; you must stay on your own bunk period! If you don't follow the rules during a lock-down you will catch a case, and any case during a lock down is a major case, which usually means a parole set off (which consists of a minimum of 1 year before you will see parole again). During lock-down commissary is closed, so if you didn't have store items set back you were hit, unless you want to borrow something from someone else for two-for-one.

On day two they called our building out, and told us to bring everything we had except our mattress to the gym so they could search our dorm. Once we got to the gym they lined us all up in front of different tables and proceeded to search through our stuff one by one. It wasn't bad especially compared to the horror stories I had heard that was happening at other unit lock downs. Once they go through your stuff, you get stripped out butt naked in front of 53 other men in the gym. They make you squat in front of them and everything. The worst part is some people don't look away, they are just watching as other grown men are stripped down, never the less there was a group of about 10 "sharks" watching everyone get stripped down. I tried to go first and just get it over with, that was the worst part.

We only got to shower twice in the 9 days we were locked down, and they gave us "Johnny's" for the majority of it (Johnny's are sack meals that always have a dry peanut butter sandwich, and a half spotted apple). I felt like I lost so much weight during the lock down. They also give you prunes or raisins once a day to keep you from getting constipated and for good reason I recommend EAT THEM! I ate them and still I wasn't right for a week after.

Good thing was that it wasn't hot in the dorm, that is always a plus. I read 3 books in the 9 days, and it was very quiet. In a sense I actually enjoyed it since most of the time it is like a mad house in there. I slept until I was actually sore because it was so quiet. I didn't get much writing done since I had a top bunk, which makes it hard to get comfortable. My main recommendation for anyone during a lock down is listen to the officers, follow the rules, stay out of the way, if you hear a lock down is coming stock up on food, and last but not least eat prunes. One more thing when they tell you take everything from your area do just that because if you leave anything behind it will be confiscated and you won't see it ever again, make sure your name is on all of your stuff. The reason is if you get the wrong guard searching stuff and names aren't present you are hit, it is your word against their and I can guarantee they will win.

I hope this has been an interesting as it is informative for you all. Stay on your P's and Q's because these laws will screw you over if you let them, and your life is on the line in the process. Keep your heads up fellow convicts and LO's.

Until Next Time, Kevin

"Natural Separation"

One universal norm that I've seen over the last few years that I've been locked up, is that people stick with their race. There are exceptions to this but normally in prison convicts stick together as far as race. It's like a law of nature almost. In 2012 when I was first put in federal custody I was put in a holding cell with over 30 people of that 30 about 25 were Hispanic men, 3 White men, and 2 Black men. As soon as we were all given our mats, blankets, and clothing, we were crammed into a small cell together. As the door closed behind us each inmate moved into sections by race. The 3 white guys were next to the black men on one side, and the Hispanics were on the other side. I sat back and observed this strange phenomenon like everyone knew where they were supposed to be.

Everywhere I've been it's been like this I can only give you a view from my perspective, because I am white. As soon as your touchdown (arrive) here, your stuff will be set down, housing will be set up then immediately you look for "your people". Usually they will lace you up with what is going on in the cell, POD, dorm, whatever the housing happens to be. This helps you out from getting into a fight, like for example which toilets are for what, which sink is for what, which TV what, and what races have what chairs, benches, tables, or whatever else. It sounds childish and immature and probably is if you never been locked up. I assure you it's very serious. It's a sign of disrespect for one race to try to impose on another races stuff (benches, tables, etc.) and can cause a situation to pop off a riot. It's weird to sit back and watch, and I told myself I wouldn't get in the mix while in county but as soon as I got to prison I just jumped right in with my helmet strapped on. Right before I left my last unit the Hispanics were mad they weren't getting to watch TV, soccer specifically on the sports channel we had. They were tripping on the black race because it was March Madness, the black dudes didn't want to compromise any. So the Hispanics pushed back and out voted the blacks to watch soccer. That was easily resolved since the black men were only 7 to 8 deep (how many there were) compared to around 22 Hispanics. These problems keep a dorm tense most of the time, you can feel it in the air and cut it with a knife. The race which out numbers others in the dorm are usually those to impose their will in the dorm.

Anyone that is a white guy who rides with another race are considered "Hook" (hoe of our kind) and are avoided by white guys who kick it with only white convicts. I am not in a family and have no interest in doing so but when you're with your people you aren't allowed to eat out of the same bowl, smoke on anything, or drink after another race. Right now I can only speak for whites but I see this with all the races. It could lead to getting "did up" or beat up by your own race if you violate these protocols. I stay to myself because I feel like there is only

I picture on my prison ID card which means no one else is going to do my time with me. Because when it is all said and done you are the one that has to tell your family and loved ones if you get a parole set-back for breaking the rules.

Racial separation is something that has gone on in prisons for as long as they have existed and will continue forever, unless we the convicts change it and that isn't going to happen. That is the way these people, the guards, and the government win, they keep us convicts racially separated. While we are busy worrying about how much the other one has or how much we hate each other the people of the criminal justice system are sitting back laughing at us fighting over the scraps. The guards would be powerless if all the inmates worked together. The law makers wouldn't be able to sneak stuff by us if we weren't haring each other for racial fueled events initiated by the government like all the white cops killing black kids. It's just smoke and mirrors while the main puppet masters in congress pull strings with the left hand as we stay fixated on the right hand. There has to be a point where we say "hey we've been fighting each other for thousands of years and it hasn't worked, why not try something different, it might just work. I have heard so many people say they were not racist until they went to prison, the government brainwashes us, and it's time we say ENOUGH IS ENOUGH! They let the guards pit us against each other and tell on each other, in the world of prison. We accept this as the norm, why? We have to look at things and understand that all of this has been designed the way it has for a specific reason. To make the rich richer and the poor poorer. That is why there is over 2.4 million locked up and the number is rising every day. Enough ranting for this blog, I hope you all enjoyed this reading, I try to tell you all what is really going on as I sit here and do my time, I hope it helps.

Until Next Time, Kevin

Chapter 4
Hello my Name Is...

I have found that through the incarceration of my son, being able to share, talk to, and encourage others helps so much in learning to heal. Although the pain is always there, sharing our stories gives others hope because they realize they are not alone.

Most of the stories you read that were submitted by the loved ones of inmates will sound so much like your own. Others you will wonder how in the world did they get through those times. I encourage you all to write your story, even if you don't share it with Inmate Sharing, you can still share it with others. Maybe in church, support groups, NA, AA, Celebrate Recovery, anywhere you can make a difference in other's lives. I always say "your story could save a 1000 lives, but it's worth telling even if only saves one".

If you would like to share your story for future publications feel free to contact us by mail or Facebook to submit.

Hello my name is Lori; I grew up with one older sister & an older brother I was the baby. I was introduced to marijuana at the age of 9 years old, as I got older and started junior high school I had started drinking, smoking skipping school and getting in trouble. I got pregnant when I was 17 and after his birth I really got wild stayed in the bars, I was raped & kidnapped by 3 men at age 18 they held me 19 hours and they ruined me. I begged them to end my life as they had destroyed me. I survived that nightmare shortly after, I got introduced to cocaine never knowing that it was going to take control of me but it did I started selling it to get my fix. I started going in and out of jail for reasons that stemmed from my drug use. My family finally just gave up and started showing me tough love, by this time I was looking at a 10-year sentence for sales of cocaine. I had completely lost me I had no idea who I was anymore, while I was incarcerated there were 3 ladies who were prayer warriors they came faithfully to minister to the inmates and I bonded with them, I knew then I had to change my life this is not what I wanted for my kids or my family anymore. It wasn't fair what I had already put them through. My mom used to cry and say "I never knew if you were dead or alive but she prayed I would survive". When I got out I went through rehab, I worked my 12 steps and thank God I made it out alive. At this point, my kid's daddy was strung out on meth so I don't know how I was strong enough to help him but I did I got him clean after he had spent 18 months in prison for selling too. It was a constant struggle our kids thought well ya'll did drugs so my son at 18 started going to jail and it got worse, he's 28 now and has spent most of his adult life in prison. It has been devastating, his dad passed away in July 2012 from cancer and it was extremely hard on all of us. I've had to deal with my son getting beat up, him doing drugs in prison and during all this my daughter got put in prison too. Most people don't understand the pain that we as family's go through but this has gotten the best of me this time.

I am now taking care of my grandchildren and they are my strength. I know there's days I want to give up completely but I can't. My babies need me, they have nobody else because everyone else has rejected them and turned their backs. My thought is if we don't support our loved ones who will?

When we make mistakes and mess up sometimes the only way for us to change is to have real support...we all make mistakes. And with addictions our loved ones don't know how much destruction they are causing, just as I didn't when I was in active addiction. I've been through a lot with my kids, my husband, also my own problems from child hood but by the grace of God I'm still standing here, still alive.

I've lost my kids daddy, my grandson Keith and so many others due to drug addictions. So I pray that maybe my story can help at least one person and hopefully more, never give up, because I am living proof you can get through this!

Hello my name is Diane and I am married to an alcoholic. He has served time twice in jail already for DWI's and now he's serving his third. He didn't learn the first two times about drinking and driving and would do it all the time until he got caught on his 3rd offense. This time they gave him more time than we ever imagined. He took a 21-year plea bargain and I pray we both don't die alone before he comes home. He is a very good man when he isn't drinking and a very hard worker. He just loves his booze too much, which in turn has destroyed our family. I do go see him every week and I will until one of us passes away or I am physically not able to. We are both in our sixties and both disabled. He doesn't need to be in prison, he needs rehabilitation. We asked the judge for a rehabilitation program and he refused said he was giving my husband the max sentence, just like he was nothing, not a human that had a true addiction rather he was sent to re-enter the prison system as just a number. It is hard most days to accept that my husband will most likely die in prison, for something that could have been prevented. As I mentioned before I really think with rehab my husband could have made it, now he will have to suffer his consequences for drinking and driving by spending the rest of his days in prison.

Hello my name is Melissa my brother was sexually abused by his scout leader as a child. He carried the secret with him for nearly a decade until he was arrested for underage drinking and had to attend counseling as part of his juvenile probation. His revelation rocked everyone but no one more so than my dad. Dad had always encouraged scouting and sometimes even insisted that my brother attend. The guilt Dad felt was incredibly profound.

During counseling, it was revealed that my brother also had mental health issues, namely OCD, depression and anxiety. He was placed on a regiment of drugs to help lessen the symptoms. When he stayed with the regiment, he would do fairly well, but he did not often stick with the regiment. Instead he found drinking to be in his own opinion more helpful. He was an alcoholic before the age of twenty.

My brother was in an out of jail from age fifteen until forty. His charges included underage drinking, drug possession, drug trafficking in a school zone and weapons charges until finally he was arrested for armed robbery. He progressed from being an alcoholic to a heroin addict in what seemed like record time. While in confinement he would find God and upon his release he would begin to go to a 12 step program with the best of intentions. The intentions never seemed to last.

In addition to jail and prison, my brother has been in and out of rehab twelve times. He has lived at half way houses three times. As a result of his last offense which sent him to prison, he detoxed from heroin in a prison cell. Each time he would go off to a court ordered rehab the family would all pray this would be the time that it would stick. It never does.

My brother, during one of his times out of jail married a girl who had just graduated from college. They were happy for approximately two months and then my brother began using heroin again. His young wife was beside herself, did not know what to do and was dragged along by my brother for nearly fifteen years before she sought a divorce. Seven years ago, when he was released from a two-year sentence from jail despite my urging to give himself time to work the program, my brother got back with his wife and she became pregnant. The relationship fell apart before my sister in law gave birth.

My niece has only known her father from visits to a prison. My sister in law would drive to the out of state location where my brother was incarcerated once a month so my niece could see her daddy. My niece is madly in love with her daddy. My niece has never known her daddy to have a job or a home other than a prison cell.

My uncle is an attorney. He has defended my brother too many times to count. If my brother had to pay for the legal services he never would have been able to and probably would have served even more jail time than he did. My uncle has regrets that he did not allow my brother to fall more quickly with the reasoning that my brother would be that much farther along now if he had hit rock bottom sooner. My uncle's theory is symptomatic of the guilt he feels for perhaps not doing the right thing to save my brother.

My mother feels my brother is making his own choices rather than being a slave to addiction and allowing his addiction to make the choices for him. She uses a tough brand of love on my brother which has at times estranged the two. My mother is reacting from a place of sorrow for what my brother's behavior is doing to my dad.

I have always supported but not enabled my brother. I feel empathy for all he has been through as a child and how it must have fundamentally changed his perception of the world. I write to my brother when he is in jail or prison and try to keep upbeat and positive. I truly believe where there is life there is hope and God can work miracles if you just allow it to happen.

My brother has gone through the judicial system and served his time alone. My parents live over a thousand miles away from my brother and I live over fifteen hundred miles away from him. We have never visited him in jail or prison. Today, my brother has served his sentence for armed robbery and has been living in a very strict half way house for two years. He is also in counseling twice a week. My brother is on parole and cannot leave the state of New Jersey. My dad fell ill this past summer and was in hospice and my brother could not come to Florida to see him. I worried this would send my brother into a downward spiral but it did not. Instead, my brother makes weekly phone calls to stay connected to any news and appears to be dealing with the situation through counseling. He is certainly talking the talk.

It has been a very long road for my dad, mom, uncle, sister-in-law, niece, sister and myself and an even longer road for my brother. There finally appears to be light at the end of a very dark tunnel. My brother appears to be doing well. He articulates he knows what he needs to do and he is going to do it this time. My brother articulates that he is over forty and needs to finally get it together. I hear my brother's words and hope in my heart that the last twenty-two years can be overcome- that he can begin to be a productive citizen, a loving father, a nephew, a brother, a son. I think to myself surely God will not allow my brother to die after all God has rescued him from in the past. Surely God will allow my brother to live a life free of drugs, alcohol, and the legal and judicial systems at least until he can live out his days as an old man.

The story of a drug addict and criminal is never one person's story. The narrative wraps itself around the lives of everyone who loves the addict/criminal. Taking a stand on someone else's story can divide a family in two. Taking a stand can estrange a family member from the very person who needs the family the most- the addict, the criminal. Not taking a stand and enabling the addict/criminal can bring even worse disaster. There are many decisions to make and I do not believe at the onset any family is prepared to make the correct decisions. We go on our gut and our heart and hope and pray our decisions will do the trick to heal the person we love so much who is suffering from so many personal demons. In the end, it truly is all up to God. As the cliché goes, one must: Let Go and Let God.

Hello my name is Neil I am 46 years old I've been in & out of jails and prisons since I was young. It started when I was young my mom and dad divorced and my dad left us I am the baby of 5 siblings, my mom was an alcoholic. It was awful in our home especially after she married a very mean and abusive man who would tie me and my sister to trees and shoot guns at us so most of the time we stayed scared to death but my sister protected me as much as possible. I don't know how I even made it through school but I graduated with honors. After high school I started hanging around friends who introduced me to marijuana and whiskey so I started spending time getting high and drunk. I got my girlfriend pregnant and I was happy until my mom passed away. When my mom passed my dad after many years came back in my life. My son, things were going ok, then I come home one day to my son's mother using cocaine. Here we go again, I started using with her and my life began falling apart. I was stealing cars and robbing my family to get my drugs running off to New Orleans to party. I was again hitting rock bottom living in ditches and eating, bathing and sometimes sleeping at homeless shelters.

In the midst of all of this I met another woman who I used for a car money drugs etc. she got pregnant and I didn't want her or a kid so I left them. Came back home started robbing more and more hurting all my family. The scary part was the "thug" life started becoming very natural to me. During this time, I conceived another son and I left him too so here I was a dope pheen with nothing but my addiction. Which became huge problems I did 10 years in prison on my grand larceny charges once then another 5 years on other charges.

One day I decided I was so tired of that life and I contacted my first wife Lori, she had always loved me. Regardless and again she was here so when I was released she came to get me and I thank God she did. She is and has always been here for me and believed in me no matter what. Lori took me back and has loved me and gave me a reason to live my life right every-day. I'm still struggling with things in life and I'm learning how to live clean and sober. I still have a lot of people to prove myself to but it's a work in progress. I pray one day my kids can forgive me because I do love them all so much. I just thank God daily for giving me another chance and if I can tell others anything it would be don't take nothing for granted and trust in God to guide you through your life daily.

Hello my name is Carmen and my journey with incarceration started when I was very young. My dad went to prison when I was only 2 years old so I don't remember a day of him not being in prison. My mom would take us every Sunday to the prison to visit our dad, me, my older brother, and two older sisters, our ages when dad got locked up were 2,3,4, & 6 yes my mom had her hands full. I remember driving there each week and sitting in line sometimes for hours to see our dad. I even remember times we drove, sat for hours, to be turned away because a lock down had gone into effect, it was hard on my mom but she always visited. I don't think she missed too many Sunday's for 17 years, my dad finally came home, in May 2013. We were all so happy even though it was kind of weird having him there because we were so used to seeing him in a totally different type setting. Always with prison guards watching every move we made, never having a family meal together, not being able to see where our dad actually lived, those were some of the many differences for a kid that goes with having an incarcerated parent. My dad was doing so good, he got a job even though he was pushing 50, he was able to save enough money for a car, and best of all he got off parole last month. My Dad has a hard time being around a large crowd or people and still does not understand anything about all the new technology but he is learning slowly but surely.

The saddest part is my younger sister started getting into trouble stealing, lying, and giving mom a hard time when she was 15 years old, she got pregnant and didn't tell mom until she was already 6 months along. Since she was young and a little over weight she was able to hide it for a while. Mom found out about her pregnancy and was so upset because she knew this meant her raising a child that would have to go through some of the things we did. My sister had gotten hooked on heroine before she got pregnant, something mom was not aware of either. Her best friend's mother called my mom to tell her about all the things my sister and her daughter had been doing, stealing, lying, doing drugs, and to top it off she heard them talking on the phone about her being pregnant, mom was so upset about all of this. She hoped for so many years we would not get into trouble because of what we had endured with our dad. We did not know at the time we found out my sister was pregnant how many complications the baby could have from the drug use. My baby sister went into labor at only 32 weeks pregnant and had to be rushed to the Emergency Room because she was bleeding very bad. Sadly, my sister died, yes she died at only 17, strung out on heroine, with a baby that would never know his mother. Our mom had to endure this pain and again without our dad, he still had 2 more years to serve when this happened.

The baby lived and my mom and dad are raising him now, they are so saddened by my sister's death, although they do believe the baby is their chance to raise a child together.

Since my dad was locked up most of our lives he didn't get to enjoy the school events, all the milestones that children have, this is a chance for him to get that, even though it is at the expense of my sister's death.

We mourn each day over what has happened, it is so hard on all of us to understand why our sister chose the life she did, but I have learned not to question things anymore, I trust in God and live life according to what I feel God has for me. My mom took us to church our whole lives so I had an understanding of how God's grace worked. It is still a daily challenge but when I feel bad days coming on I just ask God to be with us all the way through. I pray for each and everyone one of you reading this because I know you have so many struggles being the loved one of an inmate.

Hello my name is Mike and I want to tell you my story with incarceration and hope it helps others to put things into perspective for themselves. My mom was my world she was everything to me, my dad was a truck driver so I spent most of my time with my mother. She loved me so much, everything was always for me, she never left me with anyone, she always took care of me. I was an only child so me and my mom were so close. I was 10 years old and I remember my mom being sick for several months, even though she was in bed a lot she always made time for me. My mom would read to me while she was in bed, play games with me, or just hold me she made me feel so safe, she was all I had. As the months went on my mom became more and more sick until one day she told me "Mike, momma is going to die soon, I am going to go be with God in Heaven, I have something that is called cancer and the doctor told me there is not much more time left for me here". My mom went on to tell me how much she loved me and to please do good in life because she would always be there in my heart and watching down from heaven. It was only a few days later I came home from school and ran to my mother's bed to greet her like I did every day, she was very weak and could not even talk to me. I laid beside her and in only a few minutes my mom died right next to me. I remember calling momma! momma! please don't leave me please don't go. Momma I am all alone I kept yelling it out but she wouldn't wake up so I called 911 like she told me to do incase anything happened, they came to my house and took my mother away and I would never see her again. My dad was called and had to come home from his truck driving job. My dad had never really taken care of me, he always drove truck and came home maybe 3 days a month and he slept most of that. As a child I remember being so scared of what would happen to me now that my mom was gone, how could my mom be gone, I didn't understand. My dad was home a couple of weeks and he had to go to work so he went out to find a woman that could take care of me, yes only 2 weeks after my mother died my dad was searching for a mom for me. My dad brought a woman home her name was Mary and he told me she was going to be my mom now, she had a son my age, and it would be ok. Mary and her son were going to move in with us and she would make sure I was taken care of while he worked to support the 4 of us. This is where my life changed forever, Mary my new mother was very jealous of all the things in the home that were my mother's she had a yard sale and sold most of it, she was so mean to me, and her son and I did not get along. I felt so scared, lost, and I wanted to die so I could be with my mom. I was 11 now and my world had been turned upside down in a very short time. The days turned into weeks, weeks into months, and months into years until I was 17 and I couldn't take anymore so I left home, I began to use drugs, heavy drugs, I started shooting dope and it helped my pain of what I had been through the last few years as a child and now a young man. I finally found something that would ease my pain my new love METH, it made me feel so good. I caught my first case at only 19 years old. I got 10 years for a charge related to meth, I didn't have much on me but it didn't matter because it was 1984 and back then they would hang you if you were caught with any hard drugs, especially this new epidemic drug meth was becoming. In between all my madness I met a young girl that was 15 and we fell head over heels for each other, I got her pregnant and now I was on my way to prison. I only saw my son for those 10 years I served through pictures, cards, letters, and an occasional visit. His mom would bring him to see me when she could, my unit was far from where they lived so visits were far and few between. Finally, I got out and my son was 10 now and all I wanted at the time was to be a dad and give this little boy something he had longed for his first 10 years of his life. I was out for 3 months and I ran into an old friend. Yes, an old dope friend, she had not stopped even from 10 years back, she asked me if I wanted to come over and chill with her she had some good stuff. She said come on Mann it won't hurt to get high once it will be fun. That was all it took I found myself a full blown junkie again, women, motel rooms, meth that is all I wanted in my life. I wanted sex with as many women as I could get my hands on, it was a fantasy that became a reality. I started cooking dope so I had a different woman every night if I wanted. The rush of the sex, drugs, and women had become so strong I could not break away. I thought that was the best life a man could ask for, all the drugs you would ever want and women coming out of my ears, I lived this way for about 2 years until I was so out of it all the time. One of the women I was having relations with I stopped by her house unexpected and she was there in bed with some dude, I went off, I beat her so bad the ambulance was called and she was rushed to the nearest hospital. I don't know why I had so much rage but I did and it came out that day on her. I was then on the run, I left the house with all the dope, the supplies, very obvious a dope cook was living here, I took $8000 and left. I didn't get far until the cops found me at a motel where I had been staying for 8 days again shooting dope. I had met a woman and her sister the first night I got there we started using together and for the next 7 days me and those two sisters stayed in the room and did dope. Day 8 the cops busted in the door, I was taken into custody for assault with a deadly weapon and several drug charges from what they found at my house. I was sentenced to 40 years. I write these words today because I have been locked up 20 years now and I know this book is for loved ones of inmates, I wanted to share to give the loved one's hope. To let the loved, one's know those that get hooked on hard drugs especially as hooked as I was will do things that you could never imagine, it is not the person rather the drug. The things I did I am very ashamed of but I have been forgiven by God for them, although I go through hurt every-day for the pain I caused. I caused so many women pain, my son's mom most of all; I hurt a lot of people, especially my son because I was not there for him. I chose drugs over my son, people often think it is so easy for addicts to just stop but it is not that easy. I suffer from many disabilities from my drug use which by the way continued the first 10 years of my prison sentence; I used from within (yes there are drugs inside these prison walls), until one day I was so convicted by God to stop and at least use the rest of my life for some purpose. It was then I started reading my Bible and began listening to God's plan for my life. It has been almost 11 years since I gave my life to the Lord and I have accepted the fact I will be in prison most likely until I die. My prayer and biggest wish is that everyone I hurt can forgive me somehow, because for once in my life I have forgiven myself.

Hello my name is Jinny, my LO and I met in a bar, he was the Disc Jockey, he played the music. I was married and he had a girlfriend so we had no intention of hooking up. He came over and asked to buy me a drink, I said "no I'm married", he reached behind the bar to grab his dinner, he ate Chinese food, fried chicken wings and pork fried rice, I remember it to this day. A few weeks later same scenario, but this time he was eating boneless spare ribs with pork fried rice, I remember that meal too.

About a year goes by and I get into drugs and fast it becomes an addiction, which come to find out he's an addict as well. During my 1-year addiction I couldn't stand him, but he was always kind to me, making sure I was never harmed by anyone. He then does a 9 month bid in prison, during this time we lost touch with one another. Eighteen months go by which during this time he gets released and my husband left me, and he comes over one night, he says to me let me hold you, you just need to be held. I was reluctant, but laid in bed in his arms, cried until I fell asleep. He's never left me since then and I've never left him, we instantly became one, soulmates. Over the next year and a ½ we had our ups and downs, but always stayed vigilant together.

Unfortunately, addiction got the best of us and we both used together every day. Because of a dirty UA my husband violated his probation and is now serving a 7.5 sentence. Our love is strong but our faith is stronger and we will never give up on each other. Our love is a one in a kind, a true story of unconditional love.

Hello my name is Matt, my wife is in prison for 10 years, the hard part is I never knew she was breaking the law. I worked about 60 hours a week so I wasn't home much, my wife must have become bored with life. She had no-one to talk to during the day other than our children, don't get me wrong she loved them but sometimes I guess you need adults to communicate with. I started noticing my wife's behavior changing, she was moody, cried a lot, just wasn't herself. I thought it was a woman thing, it would pass, but it only got worse, so I suggested she go to the Dr. to see what he had to say about her growing depression. My wife's Dr. put her on 3 different meds, one for anxiety, one for depression, and one for sleep. She seemed to be getting better throughout the weeks. She wasn't as anxious, depressed, or sleep deprived, she expressed to me she was feeling better but still was looking for adult friends. I suggested to my wife she get involved in the community to meet people, maybe take an art class, go to exercise classes, just something to get her out and meet others.

My wife decided to take ceramic classes in hopes of meeting other adults. She met a woman and their friendship grew very fast and before I knew it they were hanging out regularly, she would be at our home almost every day when I came home after my 12-16-hour shift. This woman and my wife would stay up most of the night talking and visiting with each other, I found it a little odd my wife wasn't sleeping much again. Although she seemed to be full of energy and things were changing for her. Until one night I got up to go to the bathroom and my wife and her friend were in the bathroom together I could hear them talking but couldn't understand what they were saying. I have to admit I tried to eavesdrop but still couldn't make out what they were talking about. I proceeded to knock on the bathroom door and say hey is everything ok in there? My wife and her friend got real quiet all of a sudden, I asked again if they were ok. My wife replied in a startled voice that yes they were ok and would be right out. I hear a lot rustling around and then they both came out of the bathroom together, seemed strange but I didn't say anything. When I got up the next morning there they were at the kitchen table drinking coffee and still chatting. I asked my wife if I could talk to her in the other room, she followed me into our bedroom. "Why is she still here at 4:40 a.m." I asked. My wife assured me everything was ok and she would be leaving shortly, before the kids got up for school. Although I still thought this was a bit strange I trusted my wife and went on to work as I did every day. That was the day that would change our family forever. I got a call at work from my mother in law that my wife had been arrested? "Arrested, are you sure" I asked her, "yes I am sure" she replied. I couldn't believe what I had just heard my wife had never broken the law that I was aware of anyway. Maybe they made a mistake, what could she have done to get arrested she never even went anywhere were my thoughts at this moment, what will I tell my boss, the kids, so much was racing through my head. I told my boss there was an emergency at home and I needed to leave. I called a lawyer right away because I didn't know what else to do, I never had any run in with the police, nor has my wife. It didn't take the lawyer long to call me back and ask me if I could come in and talk to him so he could explain my wife's charges. I got right into my car and headed down to the attorney's office. He told me my wife had been charged with conspiracy and drug trafficking, I immediately told him there was no way he had the wrong person. He said "Matt, they have her on video and audio surveillance selling drugs to a confidential informant". I thought what is a confidential informant, the lawyer went on to explain what a CI was and told me he had the name of the CI but not the sale dates and times yet. The attorney told me the name and it was the woman my wife had developed a friendship with, I couldn't believe what I was hearing. So my wife's only so called friend has set her up and now she is in jail for a crime of selling and being in possession of methamphetamine. As you can only imagine the horror began that day, my wife was in county jail for 14 months before being sentenced to a 10-year federal minimum mandatory of 10 years. Although they only had 1 drug deal on audio and 2 on video, my wife had never been in any trouble or used drugs that I knew of, she was still given the max sentence for her crime.

Me and the kids (they were only 2 and 6 when this happened) now 5 and 9 visit my wife every weekend, we drive 5 hours to visit for 4. It has been very hard on our family but we are managing to have faith that she will be given a time cut for completing a required drug class. We hope and pray each day to make it through until the day she comes home.

Hello my name is Barbara my son is in jail for 25 years, he went to prison for drugs when he was 19. With only 2 years to serve we were optimistic the time would go by fast and he would be home before we knew it. Unfortunately, my son was involved in a gang riot after serving about 1 year, a man was killed during the riot. Since no-one would accept the responsibility for the actually shanking (stabbing of the other inmate) they were all tried and convicted. Seven men tried for something one did, but see it doesn't matter in the prison system it is one for all and all for one. Especially when there are tattoos on an offender that indicate they are part of a gang, as my son and the other men have. Every one of the seven men received 20 years for the brutal death of another inmate. I understand now why they call prison a concrete jungle, it is like living in a jungle, there is never an indication of what could happen. We have been doing this now for a little over 6 years, it does get easier but it never goes away. My advice to anyone who is new at this is to build your faith in God and always pray. It is a long hard road to have someone you love locked up!

Chapter 5

On the other Side of the Wire

Inmates refer to the outside world as "the free world" when they are locked up. We, the loved ones tend to start using that expression too. They are on one side of the wire and we are on the other. We are in the "free world" and they are not.

The incarcerated often look for ways to escape the reality that they are locked up and find hidden talents either they didn't know they had or haven't used. Prison gives inmates time to sit back and reflect on their lives, their current situations, their families, all the things they feel as though they are missing out on. Through poetry, letters, and writings inmates are able to express themselves in a way only they see fit. I have included several writings sent in from inmates, poetry, stories, simply words of their expressions from behind their side of the wire.

Mike Serving 12 Years
Dear Free World,

Some people just don't want to do right. Incarceration can be a time that will better yourself. Get healthy, workout, and education yourself. Most inmates want to get messed up to pass their time. Regardless the time is what you have to do. So if you care about your family or just care enough about your life to do right prison can be your chance to get your life back on track. God can help you thru all of this if you let him. These prisons are packed with negative sick inmates that will tell you all bad things to keep you down. One positive thing is you don't have to surround yourself around such inmates. Choose what you want to do wisely. The time will do itself, all you have to do is wake up and do it. Like we all say here is "do the time don't let it do you".

Thank you World,

God 1st
Family 2nd
Loyalty 3rd

Mike Serving 12 Years

Dear Free World,

We can open our minds to see what really is going on. Incarceration can really let going on. Incarceration can really let you see past your thoughts. God is working and he works thru every race, culture, every person, so don't shut your mind off to him. Prison is designed for you to crash and burn. God will never allow that if you give him the chance. I learned today talking to a man that doesn't have the same beliefs as me. We were into a deep thought conversation together and really at the end of it all, God used this man who doesn't have my same beliefs to open my mind. He really just showed me that if you don't shut down when somebody is talking and find out what's really going, it's hard to go further in life with a closed mind. Don't stay on one side of the other, stay in the middle, put everything on cruise control, God will work his way through us all. So Free World thanks again. Till next time. Better Days...

Time to work on Us,

God 1st

Family 2nd

Loyalty 3rd

Mike Serving 12 Years

Dear Free World,

Everything happens for a reason, it's all a blessing. Got to understand why we're here and change the way we think. One thing I learned is it's going to be you, not them when it gets ugly. They have turned on me and left me here to starve. There just isn't friends anymore, the ones closest to you are the ones to burn you the most. Why? Because they know everything. I woke up today thinking about how we knew this while selling drugs, but we still put ourselves thru. Our families now suffer off of our actions. But it's a lose lose because we get into situations where we might have to do this or live on the streets. So is it all worth it is the question? I have made millions of dollars and I've had nothing and I've been free and I am locked up now for 188 months' federal sentence for trafficking marijuana. I would rather be free, don't let me lie and say I didn't have fun and seen the whole world cause I did, but I put my wife and family through so much pain. So just know it is fun while it is going on, but there are always two sides to the story.

God 1st
Family 2nd
Loyalty 3rd

Kayla- Serving 5 years:

    I need the quiet so he drew me aside into the quiet where we could confide, away from the hustle and bustle where all day long I hurried and worried when I was active and strong. I needed the quiet though at first I rebelled gently but gently my cross upheld. He whispered softly of spiritual things though weak in my body my spirit took wings. I needed the quiet though jailed in prison I had to make my own bed, he made it a beautiful valley of blessings instead. It was a place to grow richer in Jesus and confide I needed the quiet so he drew me aside.

Elizabeth- Serving 10 years

Am I an angel with broken wings or the devil in disguise? Is it easier to fake the truth or just accept the lies?

Will heaven open up its gates to me or is hell my final destination?

Will I ever find eternal peace eternal peace or fool myself with manipulation?

Will I be granted salvation or had my punishment already begun?

Should I pick myself to a higher place or will I rise to fall again?

Will things ever get easier or will I always deal with complication?

Will I ever Learn to take my time or live with constant frustration?

Can I ever change who I am or am I ruled by temptation?

Is this something I must do on my own?

It's time for a revelation, am I capable of good deeds? Or is there deception in my heart.

Was I ever destined to be good or just a sinner from the start?

Am I servant to my mistakes of can I learn from the past?

Am I capable of helping others first and thinking of myself last?

Do I need to change myself or should I just accept my imperfections?

Can I find eternal happiness or will I have to live with never-ending depression?

Should I pretend to be someone else or learn to live with my reality?

Should I argue with the stranger in the mirror, or can I be content with my duality?

Will I see it through this time? Can I ever start acting my age or will I remain trapped in perpetual adolescence?

Am I willing to open myself up or am I setting myself up for a life time in jail?

Am I ready to be the women God wants me to be?

Only Time will Tell...

Chase serving 20 years

"Justified"

I was born into this fallen world a wretched sinful man afflicted with the misery of the playground of the damned, stumbling through darkness down a twisted crooked path imprisoned in the flesh waiting for the day of wrath.

Chasing feelings of pleasure sold a slave to sin.

Damnation is the price you'll pay when Satan's your only friend desolates and hopeless I fell on my knees to pray asking Christ forgiveness and salvation from the grave.

Born again in the spirit sanctified within, redeemed from the flames burning in the devil's den.

Holy mortal temple divine light shining in my soul,

sowing seeds of righteousness made the river flow.

I love my Lord Jesus Christ who was nailed to the Cross.

He died a sinner's death to save the lost.

Jesus rose the third day the first born of the dead, now I am saved and justified by the blood he shed.

Flac Serving 40 years

Mom Don't Worry

Mom don't worry and lose any sleep, I know hearing 40 cut you deep, your first born and the most troubled. But you were always there every time I stumbled.

You did your best and I can't complain, everything I put you thru only God knows your pain.

I love you like no other and everybody knows, I am a momma's boy and it shows.

You always say I can do anything if I put my mind to it, bcuz you know I am far from stupid.

Poetry is I one my talents I have to prove it. I know life doesn't stop bcuz I am in prison, but when it comes to me nothing clouds your vision.

I don't ask for much cuz of my pride, but you're the only one that doesn't seem to run and hide.

Just know that I never meant to hurt you or make you cry, all I ever wanted was to make you proud, so you'd hold your head high.

You say have faith, hope, and pray the words that get me thru every day.

So remember my laugh & picture my smile, until I am just a phone call away for you to dial.

So mom don't worry about me or lose any sleep, know I am
o.k. and my love for you runs deep.

J Bird Serving 15 years

"Woody"

As Woody and I often do
We are thinking of you.
Missing all those sexy things you do
We are thinking of you.
Your long blonde hair over your bare chest
We are thinking of you.
Your beautiful smile across your face
We are thinking of you.
Your lips so soft and wet
We are thinking of you.
The way you turn your head and look at us
We are thinking of you.
When you move your hips back and forth
We are thinking of you.
When you are lonely and need some love
We are thinking of you.
Your hands so soft stroking us
We are thinking of you.
Your legs we rub up against when we are cold
We are thinking of you.
Even when your mad and don't want to see us
We are thinking of you.
When Woody wakes up before I do I know he is thinking
about you!

Chaos Serving 10 years

"It was True"

When they told me you would leave there was no way I believed a word they said.

My baby was different in each and every way, not like all the others she was true.

I knew when I had to be away from her because it made me feel so blue.

I always knew she was in my heart and dreams, she would never leave like they swore.

That just wasn't her to walk out the door. She stuck by me through thick and thin, if people only knew where we had been.

Together for so long been through so much, I could recall each and every touch. So gentle so real I was convinced she wasn't someone you could steal.

The days went on months flew by too, my baby was slipping away from what could have been new. I wanted to change to show her she was the one, I promised her everything under the sun.

From my heart I meant these words, but she just couldn't hang on to what she thought would never be hers.

Years went by and I never heard from her again, it was true, she left what she couldn't hold, it was true she lived until she was old.

Holding on to her every thought of him, although she didn't call again, she never forgot that "It was True."

J Bird serving 15 years

"Rescued Love"

Do you Love me?

If you say it is true, I will say I love you too.

If I die before you do,

I will sit upon those heavenly stairs and wait for you.

And if you're not there on Judgement Day,

I know you went the other way.

So I will give the angels back their wings, golden halo, and other things.

And to prove to you my love is true, I will go to hell and rescue you...

Chapter 5
Surviving Relationships Behind the Wire

Surviving relationships when your loved one is incarcerated is a difficult task, but it can be done with work from both the inmate and the loved ones. Several loved ones of the incarcerated were asked questions that will arise in everyday life about ways to keep relationships strong and going, the answers are true stories of what others do to make it through together. It is very important to keep the lines of communication going in order to keep a strong relationship with an inmate. Although we are limited in how much we get to communicate with our LO because of policies and procedures of each facility, the high cost of calls, and so on, there still ways we can keep our bond strong with them. Most of the time they are not able to call and tell us what is going on. Especially when in transit (being moved from one facility to another) an inmate can get lost for up to a month or more in the system. I have seen inmates get lost in the Criminal Justice system for up to 3 months when being moved from facility to facility.

The most important thing we need to remember during this time is don't get angry if your LO hasn't contacted you, it is not their fault. Nine out of ten times it is because they truly have no way to communicate. Commissary money will freeze from one facility to another for up to weeks, so just because money was put on their books recently and then they were moved it doesn't automatically go with them like some think. Everything takes time when dealing with the system, it is so backed up it takes a long time to process cases. That is one thing we learn pretty quick is to have patience wait it out with faith.

Most of the obstacles we face along this journey someone has encountered something similar. I encourage you all to reach out join support groups and talk about ways to overcome this instead of it overcoming you. That is another way I have learned to live with the incarceration of my son is through our Incarcerated Sons, Daughters, Husbands, Wives, and Loved Ones of Felons on Facebook, it is a great group of people that truly understand the struggle of having someone you love in prison.

What is something you have done and can suggest to others to keep your relationship strong with your LO during this incarceration?

P1: "First and foremost, I have put my strength in God to the fullest. I have learned to trust God, I have learned life is so short and so precious. Most likely everyone has other family members that need them healthy and strong for them too. After my son was arrested two months and 8 days later his dad only 49 years old died of an unexpected massive heart attack. That made this even harder for us to deal with. After gaining 50lbs and developing hyper tension that I now take meds for I decided to move out of state where it was peaceful and beautiful. I gave me a totally different outlook on everything, sure I still grieve the incarceration of my son every single day, but I realize now if I don't stay strong and in good health for everyone including when he gets out in a few years what good will that do? Only make matters worse, so I try to stay positive and always remember he will come home one day and I want to be there healthy and strong for that day. Thank you Lord".

P2: "Visits, letters, cards, any kind of support just to let them know they are never alone and they are loved. When I could take the babies to see my son it always lifted his spirits, and just being there".

P3: "I can't visit regularly as I am in a different state, but when in Texas I go and see him. Writing, sending cards, trying to make him laugh. The hardest is when I HAVE to tell him bad news. I try not to tell him unless necessary, as when he lost his best friend last year. Everybody wanted me to write and tell him. It was the hardest letter I ever had to write. Thank God the Chaplain was kind enough to take the letter personally to him and sat with him for about an hour. And then one of his friends went to visit the Sunday after Jason's funeral and took my granddaughter with them, (she was only about 5 months old then) to help life his spirits. But yeah, jokes, and silly cards".

P4: "Pictures! Pictures of everything! We also read the same Bible verses every day and we are about to start reading the same books. I also include him in decisions wherever possible".

P5: "Taking all that happened positively. Accept the responsibilities that come with it. Don't blame each other for it. Pray for each other. Personally, I buy him many inspirational books. Let them always know that when one is alive, there is hope. Tomorrow will be better. Visit as much as you can and provide to his needs as much as you can. Keep the faith and let God. It keeps us going".

P6: "I write to my husband regularly; I date the letter but I send pages out dated the days that I write. This lets him know how my life, my emotions, my days are going. To keep him included on the inside".

P7: "Keeping my son up to date with what is going on, telling him the small things like his little brother won a soccer game or even something as simple as his team is taking soccer pictures. What seems like everyday life to us means a lot to them to hear about and it gives them things to talk about when they call or write us too".

P8: "I give my husband a weekly list of things that I noticed in the news, on billboards, etc. that were new for example when voice command came out on the tablets and phones, I used it all the time to type my husband's letters. I explained to him how it works, and that if you see words out of place that is most likely why. Especially for inmates doing long sentences, my husband has been in for over 14 years so Facebook and all the other social media is something he only reads about in the paper or magazines, so I tell him about new things coming out so it keeps him up to date. I have even cut out articles or pictures of new items so he can see how things are evolving really fast. I know I have had others tell me it only makes their loved one sad to realize how much is changing while they are locked up but we have to remember it is reality and I would rather him know than not".

P9: "Saying prayers for each other. I say them for him and he says them for me".

P10: "There were times especially when my husband first got locked up that he told me to move on that I didn't need to wait on him. Almost like he was pushing me away on purpose, I didn't really understand this until a lady told me at visitation her husband once told her the reason inmates say that is because that's what they expect. They hear so many stories of this happening they think maybe it will be easier get it over with. So I always remind my husband we are in this together, I love him for better or worse and I won't ever leave him. It is words they want to hear and be reminded they are loved and you won't leave them".

P11: "Even though you may not want to hurt your LO by telling them something that went on at home maybe a tragedy or just a small something you took care of. I think they should be told, it may hurt them and worry them but I feel like in the end if they find out they may be more upset that no-one told them".

P12: "I visit my daughter anytime I can get off work if I have a way I go see her, it may be a hassle sometimes for us to go see our LO's while they are locked up but the pay-off is far greater. My daughter tells me all the time if it weren't for my regular visits she doesn't know how she would cope with being in prison".

P13: "I know this day in age a lot of us barely make it financially but I still keep money on my son's books. Any amount of commissary he is so grateful that is what keeps them going especially physically because the food there is not only gross but also doesn't have too much nutrition. I think it is one of the most important things we can do is keeping money on there for them".

P14: "I can't really afford for my grandson to use the telephone while he is in prison because it costs so much, so he calls one time a week, every Sunday between 12-3 I watch the phone and I make sure and take his call. In those 15 minutes I tell him as much stuff as I can of what is happening out here in the free world. He too in return tells us what is going on there, we pass the phone around if other family are here. Often other family come and visit during that time every Sunday to catch his call. So not only does it help him get through knowing he gets to make that call and it will be answered, and the family is spending more time together waiting for the call it's a win, win situation".

P15: "Life changes so fast out here that I send pictures every month to my LO she knows the first of the month I develop them and send her at least 10 new ones, she loves to get them".

P16: "I have found that over the past 12 years since my LO has been locked up the best thing I can do is just be here for him".

P17: "I have the kids color in their color books and then they send their dad some they even send him blank copies so he can color them and send them back. I know not all units have colored pencils but we are fortunate that he does".

P18: "It may seem like a lot but I love to do it and my wife loves to get it I write in a journal everyday what is going on, my deepest thoughts, the things I want to talk about but don't want others to know. I send her a copy of the writings every week. It is good because it gives me a way to release what I have on my mind, let her know what is on my mind, and the mail that she waits for each week at mail call means so much"!

P19: "My LO told me the best part of any day when you are locked up is mail call, so I try to write or send things almost every-day. Sometimes I can't do every-day but send as much as I can and as often as I can".

P20: "Something we do that my husband really likes is we send the church bulletin that tells what is going on for the month, memory verses, what he sermon is about, etc. He says it really helps him feel connected, even though he can't physically go to church with us right now he still knows what we are learning, he studies it in his Bible so we can talk about it at visitation. It really helps to have God in the middle of our relationship our marriage is stronger now than it ever has been".

P21: "Our baby is only 3 months old and my husband just left last month so every month when I take her to the Dr. up until her 6-month appt. I make a copy of the report the Dr. gives me. It's a print out of the notes from the visit, including weight and height. My husband loved to get every month and compare how much she has grown since last one. Keeps him aware how much she is growing".

P22: "I have found over the past 3 years since my husband has been locked up it is very expensive for them to call home. What we do is he calls every Sunday between 12-4, since we only have 15 minutes, we all get 5 minutes. We even turn on a timer to make sure we stick within our 5 minutes. It gives everyone a chance to talk, and keeps it fair".

What are some idea's other than letters and cards I could send my Loved One on holidays, birthdays, etc. that makes it a little extra special?

P1: "I made a picture that has my husbands, mine, and our baby's hand inside of each other. I sent it to my husband first so he could add his hand since it is the biggest of the 3 of us. He sent it back, I added my hand inside of his, then our little boys. I sent it back to him and he keeps it in his cell area to remind himself that our hands are always together".

P2: "Look up poems for dad's or mom's print a copy and have the kids color around it. It is always great for them to be able to have things from us that have meaning".

P3: "Trace the kids hands and feet on writing paper. Then

they can write little notes in the area where the fingers and toes are. My husband compares how they grow from each one we send it keeps him aware of how fast they are growing. We do every 3 months for him, he loves it"!

P4: "Have the kids make cards with pictures they like online (example...if a child likes a certain character you can search internet for pics, save the image then they can make a card. Then write something that would be important to make sure the dad knows what the kid's interests are since they change so fast, for example their favorite colors, their friends, etc. because regular communication is important between a father and his kids".

P5: "I have personalized stationary made for my husband with our photo on some, sexy quotes on some, and different things they would like to see. You can either make them yourself or now you can order packs on Facebook just for your incarcerated LO's. You can contact Inmate Sharing for names of people that sell this stationary it is very worth getting, they love it"!

P6: "I send old pictures of me and my LO just to remind him we were in love then and we are in love now. Kind of gives him motivation to get through his sentence".

P7: "Anytime I go somewhere different e.g. on vacation, or a place I don't normally go I send a post card from there. It gives him a small glimpse of what I am talking about when I tell him about it".

P8: "A calendar that he marks off the days for another year writes little notes about them in the blocks on a calendar etc. these can be printed from Microsoft Word program".

P9: "Something we do often is print color sheets off the internet we send those to my husband he colors them for the kids and sends them back. We use characters the kids like so they can hang them in their room and be reminded of their daddy often".

P10: "My husband and our son always played baseball together it was just something they loved to do together. So our son takes the Sunday paper and goes through the sports section cuts out everything he thinks his dad would like such as articles, stats, and whatever else, he sends it to him. Then when his dad calls him on Thursday evening they call that "Baseball Talk Night" they discuss the things that our son sent and why he chose to send those. Not only does it keep them bonded but also with something they both love".

P11: "I am raising my daughter's kids while she is incarcerated there are 3 of them all girls. What we do to make sure and keep their mom in the loop of what is going on we send her a copy of their school calendars they get each month. This gives my daughter something to go on so she has ideas things she can ask them that they are doing. We also send 1 statement a month of something that changed for them that month. For example, her oldest daughter will be going to middle school next year so last week she wrote to her mom "today was the last day I will have field day". I know to some that may seem sad to remind their mother what she is missing but we believe it is more important for her to know what is happening in our home on a daily basis".

P12: "We visit my son every week, rain, sun, snow, or sleet he knows we will be there. If for some reason, we are sick we make sure and find another family or friend that will step in".

P13: "What we do to keep our relationship going is we have my sister write down what snacks she wants us to order her in a gift pack. We take it a little farther and she writes down the first word she thinks of when she thinks of the snack she chooses. It not only gives her a fun game but also helps us to stay connected".

Chapter 6
6 X 9 Life in Solitary Confinement

More and more inmates are being sent to solitary confinement in America, roughly 100,000 men and women are spending day after day segregated from other inmates. Initially when solitary was put into place it was supposed to be used for the most dangerous criminals and to keep others safe. Although, through the years it has become a place more common to the incarcerated. A small infraction can get someone sent to the Shu, riots from within the unit is another way prisoners are finding their way to seg, being affiliated with one gang or another by sporting tattoos related to a certain prison gang will also get inmates sent to solitary. For whatever reason inmates are being put into seg, inmates and loved ones claim it is hurting their mental state tremendously. The 24 hours a day away from other humans and placed in a 6' x 9' concrete cell can have a way of bending someone's mind in a bad way. You always hear about how people in seg are given an hour a day out of their cell, but I bet some of you didn't know that hour is spent outside in a cage. A cage with no bench, nothing to do but pace back and forth, next to another segregated individual doing the same thing. That is something a lot of people are not aware of.

This chapter is dedicated to those serving time in segregation, they have sent in stories, and other writings related to their experiences while being in segregation. Sometimes it's difficult to read about the conditions of seg and what it is doing to these men and women. It brings into reality what is truly going on inside that 6' x 9' concrete box.

I include this chapter regarding solitary confinement for several reasons but most of all so these inmates can be heard. Something most of them have lost hope on, is being listened to, cared about, not forgotten. These are the things that people placed in solitary struggle with, among so many other barriers that are proven to be detrimental to an inmate's mental state. When reading these writings sent in by inmates you may wonder how they can get the things they talk about if they are locked away in a cell alone? Things like drugs, medicine, food, stamps, all the things they are restricted from having. The answer to that is the staff, yes the correctional officers and other staff of prisons bring in the majority of contraband found in jails and prisons across the United States. Then they turn around and punish the inmate if anything not permitted is found in their cells. With enough contacts and money on the outside inmates have shared they can get ANYTHING they want in that prison cell.

Some of the terms you will hear when reading this section that refer to solitary confinement are:

SHU- Special Housing Unit

SEG- Segregated from others

Hole- Inmates often refer to solitary as "the hole"

Concrete Box- the area they are placed in

Cages- Cages that are roughly 10 x 15' and used to place inmates in this is their so called recreation, although there is nothing for them to do but pace back and forth until their hour is over and then back to their 6'x9' cell.

6 x 9- The average size of a solitary confinement cell

Extended- When an inmates time is solitary is extended for a longer period

Sarge serving 365 days in solitary confinement for being in
possession of contraband

I got put in the Shu for halving contraband in my
bunk area, there was a cell phone we used in the unit.
There were 8 of us and each week someone else would
hold the phone, yeah and we got it from a correctional
officer. The very person that is here to protect us is the
one providing our drugs and other contraband that is
prohibited from us having it. Well it was my week to hold
the phone, we were on day 3 of my 7 days and sure
enough they called a shake down of our area and forced us
out with no preparation. They started screaming get out
get out at 4 a.m. startled us all we got up and out fast.
The cell phone was found under my bunk so I caught the
charge that carries 18 months in seg for punishment. Sent
within 2 days of the case being filed I knew I was hit! No
canteen, no phone, no newspaper, no nothing but a
concrete wall, 5 pictures and 2 books at a time. Also
when they say we get to go out for an hour a day that is in
a cage on the rec yard. A cage like an animal's cage, that
is what you begin to feel like, an animal. With only 1-2
showers a week, pacing back and forth all day, defensive,
alone, angry, scared, mad, horrible that is how we feel
horrible. I have been here for 42 days and it seems like
an eternity, I feel like the whole world has continued
without me. I am not thought of; I am no longer a member
of society. They have stripped me of all my rights, all my
thoughts, all my integrity, they have given me a punishment

that is almost unbearable to the human mind to live through.

We will do anything here to get out of this concrete box, we will even cut ourselves and bleed all over just to get out of there for an hour. That is about how long it takes the medical staff to stop the wound from bleeding and right back in we go! The day never ends, the night seems to lurk over us always. I long for the day I am out of this hole, if I make it that long. We are humans please help us. Dearest, Conrad

Peanut serving 1 year in solitary confinement for gang tattoos

"Trapped"

Hello my name is Darin I am 28 years old born and raised in Mississippi my whole life. I've battled and took some very wrong roads that's led me to Mississippi Department of Corrections for my 2nd time serving a 24-year term.

Now let me explain to you all how I've become "Trapped" I am a former member of a gang known as Simon City Royal, at one point I was second in command over the MS Prison System at which required I put all my legal documents on a Gmail account, the government came about my information in a cell phone "2013" now 3 years later they decided to re-class me as a disruptive enforcer core member of security threat to public safety and went on to say I pose a threat to the safe and secure operation of MDOC, is here by placed in to Long Term Segregation for a term of 365 days. I was to start my new housing assignment 2-1-2016 guard came up to me and said "here give us them pants Mr. Gang Banger put these yellows' on boy it's time for you to go to SHU. Me not being a push over and used to be in prison, well as used to as anyone can be, I said "if you want these pants, come get them fat boy", yes I already knew I was gone for a year. Officer said "come on Peanut (that is my nickname) don't clown around today. I gave in and passed my black and white jump suit to get into my new bright yellow banana suite.

When you are in general population it is ran by organizations, unlike segregation is every man for himself, and God for us all so here we go "Fire in the hole" "Fire in the hole".

Shaking my head, I walk in the "Fire Zone" up the stairs all I could hear was blazing, screaming, beating, that is a regular day in SEG. I get a strange sense inside these guys don't intend to turn down. The floor walker looks so stressed out, officer looks scared to death so to my 6x9 concrete box. A single man cell first thing I do is make some homemade ear plugs, because I already know I will need them that night. I sit down on my steel bunk I hear "Peanut, say Peanut", "yeah what's up I replied who's that"? It was Trap, family from way back. "What up Fam, this is crazy they got my whole crew down here in SEG. Some I haven't seen since 2011 my 1st SEG housing unit called "Castle of Gray Skull" a very cruel and unhuman place to be.

All types of things going on in SEG like all types of items in the food, roof leaking, list goes on. It reminds me a lot of that movie "Life" with Martin Lawrence and Eddie Murphy 20,000 acres of flat land with many units of segregation. There is everything available here cell phones, drugs, knives, guns, IPad, hot spots, McDonalds, KFC, sex, you can buy anything you want if you have the money. The staff members use us to mark prices up, a $39 cell phone costs us $200, 3-piece chicken meal $25, that is why I call this place Department of Corruption.

After 24 hours a day for a month ½ of going insane, by being locked down, I attempted to kill myself from stress of not being able to talk to my family and living in a 6x9 space. I took 110 Excedrin Pills and hung myself. The LT. saw me take the pills and said "lay down see how long your heart will hold up, so I had to hang myself to try and get some type of help. I was rushed to the ER, my stomach pumped and put on 24/7 oxygen for 2 weeks. I realized after this God has a plan for me, even though I was released back into segregation this time to the death row unit AKA 29-J. Placed on the row with all these guys waiting to die, but these were the best guys I seen in a long time. My guy Kung Fu been on death row 14 ½ years was really great to meet him, he was serving 3 death sentences well after 2 weeks I was moved to another unit which is a crazy house. The SHU here is wild, floods, fires, shit shakers, yard call comes 5x a week, we are put inside a 10x10 cage, yes this is what they call rec for us. It is our only taste of freedom. Couple of guys a day try to kill themselves here, lots of pepper spray is used here. The food is a little better than dog food but not near as good as school lunch. The cellie right next to me threw spoiled milk and feces on an officer today, they waited 8 hours to go into his cell to clean things up. Because of his actions we were all punished, we didn't get our 1 hour outside in the cages. They also took an extra 2 hours to feed us they wore shields to feed us which I guess is the reason for the delay. They often run into our cells sometimes 10 deep (means 10 officers) and start yelling stop resisting, stop hitting us, this is their way of using force by accusing us of resisting, how can one man with 10 guards surrounding him in a 6x9 area resist? It is another way to justify our punishment and use force on us. I have seen so many beaten, kicked, spit on by guards all while being cuffed.

I've found out recently my new parole date is September 2016, maybe I will be able to spend Christmas with my family this year, if so it will be the first one in 8 years straight. I have been blessed to have Inmate Sharing on my side, the director Jodi had been by my side with much support. That has helped me so much because the devil has really tried my luck through this SEG time. Only the strong survive here the bad part is they say to keep 2 knives on you at all times in the MS prison system, seen 2 guys get killed in riots, this here is crazy living but I know I won't be here forever, but what about the rest of them?

Otis serving 7 years in solitary confinement

Hello my name is Otis I have been in solitary confinement for 4 years. I was diagnosed with bi-polar several years back when I got to prison it was too hard to get the medication the Dr. had me on so I wasn't given anything for my disability. I started to lose it shortly after I was put into SEG, hearing voices, seeing things I know wasn't there, sweats, severe anxiety, and the list just keeps going on and on.

I will never forget the day I was put into the SHOO it was like another planet, a place no one ever wants to be! I had fear overcome me shortly after I had been placed there, thinking what if I die and they don't come down here to check on me and don't know. What if I get sick, need some help, there will be no-one here to help me? The first tray I was served after I got here looked like mushed cat food, I wasn't hungry anyway so I didn't eat it. I learned real fast that was a big mistake, because when I sent it back during tray pickup I was told to get ready for what was to come, because food was not to be wasted in segregation. I didn't even think it was food, it didn't look like something anyone would ever want to eat. The punishment was the next meal I got soggy bread with slop on the top, they call this "The Log", and if you don't eat the log they will serve it to you until there is no more waste. I learned real fast to flush any food I wasn't going to eat because eventually I was going to have to eat slosh is what I call it.

Sometimes an insect comes into my cell that gives me something to do, something to talk to, yes I name the insects and try to keep them alive. It is the only life there with you although it is a bug you can find ways to entertain with a simple little creature. Life is looked at so different when you're in SEG a small touch of freedom even if it's through a bug is better than being alone. I don't know how long I will have to stay here, they don't tell you anything but how pathetic you are, a waste of air, the guards don't care if we die either because that is one less menace they have to deal with. Seg is part of my life now sad part is I don't know how I will feel about going back into general population with other men all around me, that day seems too unreal now. When you are locked in a 6x9 concrete wall cell with no window it tends to put a toll on you and make it where death seems like it would be much easier.

Jay serving 10 years in solitary confinement

Your letter it really did what it was sent to do. It gave me HOPE or should I say it strengthened and kept alive my hope. That is the only thing that keeps me going. I do read my Bible daily and am now a True Follower of the Holy Bible, and I know why you wrote me, you don't really even know me and I don't know you. We have never been friends you have no reason to write me a letter. There is at least "1000" so called friends, people that should have wrote that letter. I've had 2 friends write to me one time the first month I was gone and never heard from them again. And Lisa...)-: well I blew that, worst mistake of my life! Well second worst the first was thinking I was fooling God, I was living Galatian 6:7 but never again.

The Lord has opened my eyes like never before, ok let me say it again I don't know why you wrote. Because God hasn't made it fully clean to me... YET but I do know who made you write, or guided you. This I know God will be successful in whatever he is trying to do here.

Let me tell you a little about my everyday life, I have been in AD SEG ever since I got locked up. I am in a 6 x 9 cell, solid concrete. It is really like the size of a small bathroom, I got a metal bunk, toilet, sink, 0- and a BIG METAL DOOR with a little doggie door at knee level 1" x 6" that is where they put my food in at. I am locked in here alone 5 days a week 24 hours a day and on the other 2 days I have the opportunity to come out of my cell and go to a recreational cage alone. The rec area is.... Well it's a cage 20' x 15' (it's not really square) for 2 hours a say on those 2 days, so I am only in my cell for 22 hours those two days. That is if I decide to even go out because there is nothing in the cage to do, walk in a little circle.

So in saying that I am saying all I have to do all day everyday 365 days a year for 3 years now is sit in my cell and read God's word and study it and get to know him. AMEN!

Yes, it is a blessing for the most part but with no one to talk to or share with or learn with or ask a question to... I wish I could make every Christian go into a cell like I have been in only 30 days with only a Bible. It will change your whole life! It has been a life changing experience far beyond what you could ever imagine. I wouldn't want no one to have to do it for over 90 to 180 days.... THREE years is a little too long. They tell me I am going to have to stay here for 10 years. It really messes some (most) men up in Bad Way!

It messed me up bad the first 30 to 90 days, but thank God I've continued daily in his word. Like I said the hardest part is not having no one to talk to or share with. I do any and all the Free Bible Study there are available to me through the mail. I am indigent so the state limits me to only 5 mail outs a month.

Again, thank you your letter has truly touched me it has given me a new hope, The Lorde is at work here and I don't know if I will ever hear from you again. But be rest assured you are your family will be in my prayers daily, May God Bless you as you have blessed me... Psalm 37:4, oh one last thing you said besides hope that has stuck in my head, "Make Peace with Yourself" Well I thought I did but... Well I am not sure if I have yet. Thank you so much for writing God Bless You!

Big Red in solitary confinement for 5 years

I have been locked up in solitary for 4 years, I was given 6 months in the Shu for fighting on the yard. If you are approached by another dude the thing is you have no other choice but to fight. I was given 180 days because they considered it a riot since there were multiple fights and known gang members were involved. Well those 6 months have turned into 5 years now. You see when you are in SEG (another name for this hole), if you have any disciplinary write ups more time is added. I had a tooth ache so bad for weeks I had complained and complained to guards I need to see a dentist. You see though they don't care down here in SEG they yell back things like "shut up", "go to sleep", I even had a guard tell me maybe I will die and that is one less he has to deal with. This one night my tooth had gotten so bad my face was swollen they wouldn't help me so I decided to try and pull it myself. I took a plastic fork they gave me with my breakfast that morning and made a tool.

I started digging into my tooth and not only did it get worse but started to bleed everywhere. By this time, I was in so much pain I would have rather been shot in the head and taken out of my misery. When the guard came around I started screaming obscenity to him in desperation of his help to get me medical attention. I started banging as loud as I could for hours and still got no response other than yelling the usual slurs by CO's. So I finally just said ok I will kill myself and then they have to come get me but now it wouldn't be for a dental visit it would be to carry me out in a body bag. I started getting my blanket ready to tie to the top of my bunk and attempt to hang myself. I was successful in the hanging part but the CO's must of caught wind to what was going on. He sent for an entire team with shields to come in and attempt to save me. They saved me alright I was taken to the hospital where I stayed for 5 weeks due to multiple brain problems from lack of oxygen.

After my recovery I was sure they would put me back into general population since it was apparent I couldn't stay in SEG anymore, I was going crazy, literally crazy. I was wrong instead they wrote me up as a threat to general population and placed me in Administrative Segregation for a term of 5 years. I was being punished for trying to kill myself, rather than given help I was left helpless! They didn't ever fix my tooth I just had to wait for that thing to crack enough that it came out in pieces on its own.

The depression here in SEG gets worse than anyone could ever imagine, there are weeks you don't go outside because of the weather. Something a lot of people don't realize though that hour a day they claim we get outside is a lie and a joke. We are put into a cage that is about 10x15' most of the time right next to someone we hate. No chair, nothing but a concrete slap inside a cage, it reminds me of the animals at the zoo. The worst part is if you are next to another inmate you have rivalry with things can get real heated fast. Like I said though a lot of the time we don't even get rec because I am here up north in a cold state where it gets below zero. One time I went 5 months without going outside at all that when I went out it felt like the sun was going to blind me.

Cookie served 6 months in solitary confinement for getting caught trading commissary items

Spending 6 months in solitary really changed my life, it makes you feel like your whole world is being torn out from under you. Being in prison is bad enough but getting put in the hold is really bad. No phone calls, no canteen, no interaction at all with anyone but yourself and God. I did read my Bible a lot while I was locked up alone, but even that gets tiring. You can only sleep a certain amount of hours a day. I usually averaged about 18 sometimes even 20, because when I was awake there wasn't anything to do but pace in a 6' area.

The minute I stepped foot in that cell I felt like the world stopped, it feels like a place of no other, a place of despair, there is no escape at all. It is like being in a country and not knowing the language. I only got 1 shower a week for 5 minutes, it was such a process, you have to be stripped down anytime you come out of your cell. It gets so hot in there sometimes too you almost feel like you can't breathe. Like you are smothering. Then on the other end of the spectrum it is freezing in the cold months and you are only allowed 1 blanket and its paper thin. There is one small door that they slide the food tray through and every night when the sun went down we would all sing. There were 8 of us on the hall and even though we couldn't see each other just to hear another human was what got me through such a rough time. At night we would sing old rock and roll and play trivia. The first person to name the song got to go first the next round. Anything to keep us sane, but it isn't always that cooperative, you always have them bad apples up in SEG. Those guys that want to scream and yell the whole day and night. I know they do it because they are going crazy and crying for help, but then I also know they know too no-one is coming for us. That is why I don't understand why these dudes spend so much time begging for help. When you are in solitary it is you and God no-one else is going to help, I learned that pretty quick after I got here.

Flip served 8 years in solitary confinement

There is no such thing as boredom in a solitary confinement cell it is way beyond that, I would have to call it desolation, helplessness, despair, the worst feeling other than death you can feel. Sometimes I wonder if you even feel after being there for so long. I spent 8 years, 14 weeks, 3 days, and about 2 hours locked away in a 6x9 cell alone. Yes, alone, you can't imagine how it feels to totally be alone, yes I believed God was with me too. But sometimes you just can't feel him, for whatever reason. I don't understand how I could have been placed in solitary confinement because a guard was killed on my floor and I happen to be in the area it happened. I didn't even see who did it, I was watching TV in the area they call the day area my back was turned. All I could remember is the loudest scream I ever heard in my life, well until I got to solitary that is. The screech was so intense that it cut to the bone, I turned around all I could see was blood all over the floor and other inmates surrounded around a body. The body happened to be of a guard that was a total jerk to everyone. Me and him had gotten into a little situation a week before, he wanted to take my candy because he said I had more than what was allowed. I cussed at him a little and went on, no big deal, nothing huge.

When this incident happened in the day room because I was there and had beef with this CO automatically I was accused. I was put into a concrete hole to rot. I felt most days I was rotting; I couldn't believe my life had ended up this way. I was originally in prison for drug charges now I am serving life for a crime I didn't commit. I often wonder why me, why was I picked to suffer this way, then I remind myself as the Bible tells me in Romans, we are to suffer as Jesus suffered for us. The way to get through for me is to always remember this life is temporary. One of these days I won't have to put up with any of this stuff, or any of these people.

Peanut serving 1 year in solitary confinement

I just wanted to write a few lines back to you to
say thank you so much for your support. Every letter is
something like freedom I've been really stressed down and
out, but I read my letters and it reminds myself I've got
this. I am bi polar and I have ADHD I'm really active so I
walk back and forth all day from the door to the wall it is
9' across only about 5 of it available to walk. There is
beating on the walls all day long and night by other inmates
locked away in SEG, also fires, floods, pepper spray, it all
drives me crazy. I try to block it out but man it's hard.
There is this one kid they call him JUV he is only 20 can't
read or write, he had mental illnesses and been in here for
4 years solid. Most of the time I would love to chock him
but I feel sorry for him. He sells all his food, soap, tissue,
clothes, anything he has. He doesn't shower, eats food off
the floor that folks throw away. He begs all night for
anything; scraps, cigarette butts, weed roaches, and any
kind of pills. He loves them Benadryl's, he will snort
anything, I mean anything. These guys are so cruel to him
they put stuff in food and give it to him on yard they know
he is starving, they put nasty stuff in their boogers, piss,
feces, it is so mean. I been here over a month and all I
seen him wear is a long t-shirt that thing is filthy too. He
hasn't changed or showered at all since I been here.
These guys will crush pills and tell him snort them, then
they laugh at him when he starts talking crazy from the
affects it gives him. He never sleeps either he just cries

every night, all night long begging for help, and this correctional officers just laugh, it really makes me sick! I know how to maintain myself though and I can't wait for these people here to be exposed.

I just want you and the other folks that wrote me to know I appreciate it so much. I am having a hard time getting stamps to write them back, we are restricted in here and can't buy anything including stamps. I am really hoping I make parole in a couple months so I can get out of this hell hole I am in. Like yall told me in my letter it is not how many times you fall it is about how many times you get back up that matters. I plan this time in bettering myself, going to college making something of my life this time. I have a 6-year-old daughter that is my life she is my motivation to do right and stay out. My momma too, I love her so much and don't know what I would do without her. Please tell everyone thanks again and when I get down which is most of the day every day I pull out the letters they wrote and it motivates me to keep going. God Bless You All, Peanut

Sticky served 3 ½ years in solitary

"I served more than three years in solitary confinement, with four stints in two prisons. His daughter was born while he was in solitary.

The very first moment that I went into solitary confinement was very fearful for me. It was just fear of the unknown: you walk into this building and the lights are so dim you can barely see, everything is so dark. All of the officers, they just look so much more crazy than everybody else outside of the solitary confinement, they have long beards and long hair. And you hear a lot of noise, a lot of people banging and yelling and screaming and kicking and you have absolutely no idea why they're doing it until you get in a cell.

Sometimes my daydreams took me to places where I didn't think my mind could go. I've been in solitary for so long that it was hard for me to differentiate real from fantasy, because I would daydream for so long that I've had officers knock on my cell door and I will completely block them out and they would have to literally kick the door until it shakes and then I will realize, you know, somebody's there and I will turn around and speak to them.

After my release from prison the majority of the things that have taken place in solitary confinement have, really stuck with me, but the one thing that I can point out the most is being able to interact with a lot of people at one time. It's very hard for me to interact with more than two or three people at the same time without feeling somewhat paranoid or sometimes I feel like I'm having an anxiety attack. I don't like to go places, my wife can't touch me at night anymore, when I am in a tight place I start to have heart racing and feelings of passing out. Solitary confinement ruined me, it stripped the person I was, it left me with scars so deep they may not ever heal.

Chapter 7
Time Served

Although some offenders reoffend others are given such hefty sentences they don't get out to reoffend, and then there is the small percentage that succeed by overcoming the criminal justice system. According to a Pew study completed in 2008 over 50% of offenders re-offend, they go back to prison. Some only go back once where as others go back time and time again, mainly for non-violent drug charges. When inmates are not treated for their addictions, rather let out of prison with no job skills, a criminal record, and a drug addiction, that alone is set up for failure.

I have seen time after time inmates being required to work, go to classes, go to probation/parole, attend support groups, and the list goes on. It is very hard to work and also balance the requirements of parole. I am not saying it's acceptable for inmates to return to prison, what I am saying is most of the time their backs are up against the wall. They don't stand a chance from the minute they hit the streets. Released back into their old neighborhoods, with old friends, no job, and most have no support system. This is a set up for recidivism before they are even released.

Bob-Served 13 years

A year ago today I was sitting behind the gates of hell waiting and watching time tick, tick, tick away, in anticipation waiting until midnight when I would become a free man. I was released from hell at 12:01 a.m. after doing 13 long years. Now I sit at a job, with a car in the parking lot, a beautiful woman that waited for me, life is great, do we heal from incarceration is a question I am asked a lot, my answer is if we want to. Just like any other trauma in life do we heal from it, yes if we want to we do. I want to thank my family and God for believing in me and trusting me, most of all loving me for who I am. I am who I am today because of what I went through which I would like to believe I am a better man.

The key to this is what we choose, there will be set backs, hard times, and best of all rejection from society because we are the population most don't want to give a chance, we are often looked at as the plagued population, the criminals. I didn't let that stand in my way, I refused to take no for an answer and if you want to change your life and merge back into society you too will need to do the same. Fight for what you believe don't give up and definitely don't take NO for an answer keep on keeping on until something breaks because it will, I am living proof it will. So the answer to the question do you heal after being locked up? In my case yes you do.

Blake- Male Inmate Served 12 years:

Got out of prison a few months ago after serving a 12 year bid, been a rough transition back into society. BUT, I am PROUD to say that I finally found myself a JOB! I've been managing to feed myself by playing my guitar for a little cash now and then, but now that I'm working I pretty much eat for free which is AMAZING. I feel so blessed. Phase One: COMPLETE. Phase Two: Back to school. I'm so happy life is beginning to look up for me, I just want to spread the joy. If you're out there busting your rear and feeling like nothing's working, just hang in there! Good things will definitely come to those willing to work for them. I love you all, have a wonderful day!

<u>Carlos Served 7 years</u>

Re-sentenced to 5 more years, released on mandatory supervision for 3 years.

First 60 days were torture. No family to call. Decided to go to a town I didn't know anyone since I wasn't very successful from staying away from my old crew. Wanted a new chance, New town, new people. Parole requirements and officer's requirements were like contradictive and confusing. After 45 days I went to my PO and asked to be sent back as it was difficult to find a job and a place to call home. He refused. That same night got ☎ call for job interview next day. Got a ride with our public transportation for my interview. I couldn't find place. Too ashamed to ask for help so I gave up looking for the place about an hour later. I went to a bathroom in Wal-Mart sat in stall and cried and told God thank you for making me see how stupid I am to believe this was true. Washed my face and started to walk back to the bus stop, I passed a convenient store that had a help wanted sign in the window. I thought well it can't hurt go inside and ask to fill out an application. When I went in the manager was there behind the counter I asked her for the application and she asked me what hours I could work, I told her I would work anytime she needed me to. I was hired on the spot without even filling out an app. That was 5 months ago and to this date my boss does not regret her choice. I am in the process now of opening a recovery house for reentry for those with aggravated case's that no other so called ministries want to accept. We accept those shunned by family for what they may call shame to family. I know God was there in that Walmart bathroom stall that day and he heard my cry for help, he helped me right then. Maybe you are ready to give up hope, you been turned down for jobs because of your record, or whatever is going on in re-entry but I can say one thing faith in God always comes through. God Bless you all!

Rocky Served 11 years

They consider me a successful person who has reentered society. I never should have been in prison. Yet, I guess I am viewed as successful because I have been published, spoken at some high profile events and I abide by my "outpatient" commitment rules for supervised release.

I think that my reentry has been one joke show after the other, but because of the high profile nature of my case and my mental illness and suicidal ideation, many people in the field of advocacy here in DC were waiting for me to get out to support me. I reached out and they reached back. I did not have to apply for a job, one was created for me--although it is part-time. After I was abused by my roommate that I had been partnered with through program sponsored by the Department of Behavioral Health (DBH) and filed a complaint, they had me evicted and I became homeless for two months. I lived on couches in hotels and in a very volatile situation with one of my brothers who is an abuser. Then my boss confronted DBH (Department of Behavioral Health) and threatened to expose them so I got a voucher which allows me to live any-where in the city as long as the apartment does not cost more than the allotment of the voucher. I pay 30% of whatever my salary is. However, I have a community that cares about me. I have struggled. I struggle. I do not feel like I should be on a poster for the BOP stating I am a success story because during my incarceration I almost killed myself several times. My therapist has been a gift. In DC we have Community Support Agencies for people with mental illness and because of "who I am" I was partnered with the best one here and had an amazing case manager. I found a church that I love and attend regularly. And I have started writing. Reentry is an ongoing process. I was devastated two weeks ago when I was denied an apartment because of my "criminal history" but then Grace stepped in and HUD released the new guidelines and I got the apartment. But I struggle. I miss my son. I miss my son so much and he comes in and out of my life. We are Facebook friends but he is not ready to see me and I have been home for a year and a half. I guess the fact that I am fighting to live after surviving prison and all the abuse that comes with incarceration means I am reentering with some degree of success. I think shaking off shame and saying I stand on truth and speaking my truth, writing my truth and advocating for women like me is probably what I can say is why my reentry is a success.

Christine Served 14 years

  After serving 14 long long long years in prison I was finally released almost 2 years ago. I have to say at first it took me months to just get used to the fact I could come and go as I wanted, I could eat when I wanted, I could sleep, I could enjoy the simple things we miss so much when we are locked up. Just being able to put salsa on your food, or salt and pepper is a luxury to an inmate. I am so great full to be out of prison, although it is a tough road. When I first got out I had plans to get a job, save up for a car, be able to go places I missed out on for all those years. I had so many plans but none of them went through like I thought they would.

  It was really hard to get a job but someone finally gave me a chance. I am a short order cook in a restaurant because of my felony record it is hard to get people to hire me. I took the first job that was offered to me after applying for what seemed like 100's. I haven't been able to save any money because as you can imagine a short order cook doesn't make much and parole requires me to pay each month fees. To get through without wanting to use substances, I go to NA. Narcotics Anonymous was such a blessing when I was locked up and I am so thankful I continued my step work and found a great group to call home. Re-entry is much harder than I ever imagined, but by the grace of God and never giving up things are starting to look much better. When I start to get down I remind myself that freedom alone is enough to be thankful for. I may not have everything I thought I needed but I have everything I want. Life is hard no matter if you are locked up or free so my motto is "make the best of just being free", because until you have it taken away you have no clue how precious time really is. I refuse to waste one more second of my life.

Chapter 9
Prison Art

Inmates are limited on things they can do while being locked up. Some of the best artists I have ever known are inmates. It seems like their talents come out when they are locked up. They have more time, to devote to their art when they are locked up with nothing much to do.

The artist comes out in a lot of men and women that are incarcerated. So many amazing artists are locked up and using their artistic abilities not only for something to do, but also as therapy for their minds. Inmates use their art in several different ways, they send letters and cards with art done for the reader. Offenders have also found a way to trade art for commissary items, and other things that gives them financial gain while being locked up.

Inmates sent in art for us to publish and share with our readers. We would like to encourage others to do the same, we are working on a book now that is only for prison/jail art and hope to get some nice pieces to include.

Her beauty flows, I will never forget her face, her lips, and

love...

The Desires of my heart leave me wounded, addicted, and

tormented.

About the Author

Dropping out of high school and having a son at only 15 years old was the start to a very difficult life for Jodi. She chose to persevere when her son's dad received a hefty prison sentence in the late 80's for drug charges. Left with a 3-year-old, no education, addicted to drugs, and homeless, Jodi knew it was time to change her life around.

Going back to school to get her G.E.D. then going on to college completing a Bachelor of Science in Criminal Justice. Jodi was always interested in the field of criminal justice however not to punish offenders but rather advocate for them.

Years later with two kids and a single mom Jodi met her husband John they have been married for over 10 years and have 2 children of their own. When her youngest was born she decided to go back to college to get her Master of Science in Higher Education with an emphasis on criminal justice. After teaching school for several years Jodi decided it was time to move on to college level teaching. Therefore, she chose the criminal justice subject as her concentration.

Then in 2013 her and her family's life took a twist, her oldest son was arrested on federal charges, facing a possible life sentence. As her son awaited trial in a filthy jail, she began to reach out as a way to cope; she spoke to men and women in prison and began a Facebook support group for loved ones of prisoners. To date: Jodi writes to inmates all over the world and gives them a glimpse of hope as they serve their time "Locked Up".

"Locked Up"

We never wanted to see our loved ones "Locked Up."

The pain we face when our love gets caught on the other side of the wire.

The side where no-one wants to be, only waiting to be set free.

Set free from despair, where the unknown takes place and it seems as no-one there has a care.

Not a care for your thoughts, nor your sorrows, they all battle with the scars of being "locked up".

We all wait until the day the gavel hits down; the judge sentences our loved one with a frown.

A frown to another one locked away, his thoughts now owned by the system. The only choice now is to wait day after day.

Not only is he locked away, but also his sons, daughters, husbands, wives, and loved ones are also led astray.

I say to you today, this won't last forever, you may be "locked up" now but one day we will be together...

Jodi Rose/Inmate Sharing

I would like to encourage you all to find strength in the word of God when you get down about your LO being "Locked Up". It is hard I can honestly say I understand, although I always say all of our pain is different even if our situation is the same. The best thing you can do during this time is to keep faith, learn patience, and reach out to others in your situation. A lot of time we try to get through the incarceration of a loved one alone when we don't have to or need to. There are many support groups on Facebook, we would love for you to join us, we understand and we care. My hope is this book helps to put things into perspective, give encouragement, gain more knowledge of the cj system and what to expect, and helps you in any way possible. If you would like to submit stories, art, poetry, information to be published in our upcoming writings feel free to write us at our address in the front of this book, and like us on Facebook.

God Bless You All, Inmate Sharing

www.ingramcontent.com/pod-product-compliance
Lightning Source LLC
Chambersburg PA
CBHW021427170526
45164CB00001B/134